indian
EVERY DAY

indian
EVERY DAY
LIGHT, HEALTHY INDIAN FOOD

Anjum Anand

headline

First published in 2003
by HEADLINE BOOK PUBLISHING

10 9 8 7 6 5 4 3 2 1

Cataloguing in Publication Data is available from
the British Library
ISBN 0 7553 1200 7

Set in Helvetica Neue and Scala

Designed by Isobel Gillan

Photography by Siân Irvine

Home Economist Tamsin Burnett-Hall

Colour reproduction by Spectrum Colour, Ipswich

Printed and bound in France by Imprimerie Pollina s.a. - L88484

HEADLINE BOOK PUBLISHING
A division of Hodder Headline
338 Euston Road
London NW1 3BH

www.headline.co.uk
www.hodderheadline.com

CONTENTS

A note on measurements

Equivalent weights are approximations only. It is therefore not a good idea to switch between metric and imperial in one recipe; stick with one or the other.

Unless stated otherwise, all spoon measurements are level.

1 teaspoon = 5ml   1 tablespoon = 15ml   1 cup = 250ml

Conversion tables

weight
10g = $\frac{1}{4}$ oz
15g = $\frac{1}{2}$ oz
25g = $\frac{3}{4}$ oz
30g = 1 oz
40g = $1\frac{1}{2}$ oz
50g = $1\frac{3}{4}$ oz
60g = 2 oz
75g = $2\frac{3}{4}$ oz
80g = 3 oz
100g = $3\frac{1}{2}$ oz
125g = 4 oz
150g = 5 oz
175g = 6 oz
200g = 7 oz
225g = 8 oz
250g = 9 oz
275g = $9\frac{3}{4}$ oz
300g = $10\frac{1}{2}$ oz
350g = 12 oz
400g = 14 oz
450g = 1 lb
500g = 1 lb 2 oz
600g = 1 lb $5\frac{1}{2}$ oz
700g = 1 lb 8 oz
800g = 1 lb 9 oz
1kg = 2 lb 4 oz

volume
30ml = 1 fl oz
50ml = 2 fl oz
75ml = $2\frac{1}{2}$ fl oz
85ml = $2\frac{3}{4}$ fl oz
100ml = $3\frac{1}{2}$ fl oz
125ml = $4\frac{1}{2}$ fl oz
150ml = 5 fl oz = $\frac{1}{4}$ pint
180ml = 6 fl oz
190ml = $6\frac{1}{2}$ fl oz
200ml = 7 fl oz
250ml = 9 fl oz
300ml = 10 fl oz = $\frac{1}{2}$ pint
350ml = $11\frac{1}{2}$ fl oz
375ml = 12 fl oz
400ml = 13 fl oz
450ml = 15 fl oz
500ml = 18 fl oz
600ml = 20 fl oz = 1 pint
650ml = 22 fl oz
700ml = 23 fl oz
750ml = 25 fl oz
800ml = 28 fl oz
1 litre = 35 fl oz
1.2 litres = 40 fl oz = 2 pints
1.5 litres = 48 fl oz
1.8 litres = 60 fl oz = 3 pints
2 litres = 70 fl oz
2.5 litres = 80 fl oz

length
3mm = $\frac{1}{8}$ inch
5mm = $\frac{1}{4}$ inch
1cm = $\frac{1}{2}$ inch
2cm = $\frac{3}{4}$ inch
2.5cm = 1 inch
4cm = $1\frac{1}{2}$ inch
5cm = 2 inches
6cm = $2\frac{1}{2}$ inches
7.5cm = 3 inches
8cm = $3\frac{1}{4}$ inches
10cm = 4 inches
13cm = 5 inches
15cm = 6 inches

temperature
160°C = 310°F = Gas $2\frac{1}{2}$
170°C = 325°F = Gas 3
180°C = 350°F = Gas 4
190°C = 375°F = Gas 5
200°C = 400°F = Gas 6
220°C = 425°F = Gas 7
230°C = 450°F = Gas 8

PREFACE

NOT ANOTHER COOKBOOK! Well, it is and it isn't. This cookbook is not about restaurant food, nor is it about comfort food. It's not a Larousse Gastronomique of Indian ingredients, nor is it a journey along the meandering banks of a culinary Ganges. But it does have facets of them all. This book is not about being the best cook or host, although it can take you a little closer to all these ideals.

It is about exploring the familiar as well as introducing new ingredients to your everyday meals. It is about demystifying Indian cuisine and its explosive flavours. It will change your perceptions of Indian food so that you will contemplate eating or cooking this way at any time of the day and on any occasion.

The recipes here are a modern take on authentic home-style Indian recipes. I employ healthy cooking techniques, with modern and convenient ingredients, to create a variety of dishes, both spicy and mild. I use one or two main flavours to enhance, rather than drown out, the star ingredients, but I have also included a good helping of curries for the diehard fan.

This millennium is about healthy eating. No more starvation diets, no more elimination diets, no more raw food, no more colour coordinated diets, no more, no more . . . Just say no! This millennium is about feeling good about yourself. And as we all know, food can make you feel great or it can make you feel rotten. Whether too much or too little, food can cause havoc with our psyches as well as our bodies. Food is fuel. We have to eat it so it may as well be tasty. For me, the key word is moderation. A little of what you fancy and a lot of what you need is the way to go. This is the way I eat and this is what my book is about.

More times than I can remember, people say to me: healthy *Indian* food? Too good to be true, I hear you think, given our exorbitant national consumption of butter, cream and sugar. Many would go along with the Oxford University debating society in dismissing the healthy virtues of Indian food. The general consensus is that it is too heavy to eat regularly and too complicated to cook. So on the whole we 'indulge' in a 'curry' on special occasions. Even many Indians stay away from most of their national dishes for fear of their bodies going, literally, pear-shaped!

However, the fact is that home-style Indian food can be healthy, fun and light; it can be casual or formal; it can be a meal or a snack; it can be comfort food, diet food, traditional or modern. I am not being contradictory; it really can be any or all of these things. To me it is one of the world's greatest cuisines because it caters for non-vegetarians, vegetarians and vegans, as well as fussy eaters and those with food intolerances.

These dishes are a far cry from those you experience at your fave Indian restaurant. You will never have to avert your gaze from the pool of fat that collects lovingly in the lap of the reposing serving spoon. It is a world apart: lighter, often aromatic rather than spicy, replete with fresh ingredients paired with different combinations of spices to create a variety of dishes. They may seem familiar but there is a definite difference. As with any home-style cooking, it is simpler, easier, healthier and tailored to suit your own palate. Try it and you will see what I mean. *Indian Every Day* will colour your daily life with a vibrancy of aromas and flavours.

inspiration: my story

You may never have heard of me but my story will no doubt sound familiar, as the desire to be healthy transcends race, religion, age and gender. We are all united in our intention to eat well and similar stories of both success and frustration echo from around the world.

My 'gourmand' gene and love of my mother's cooking (bless her) got me into this mess in the first place. By the time I was eighteen I was carrying around umpteen extra pounds (around seventy-five, in fact, give or take a few) and I felt pretty uncomfortable with it. I tried every faddy, mainstream, high-protein, high-carbohydrate, low-fat, no-fat, all-food, no-food diet there was to shift the weight. But as soon as I resumed my old habits, like bad pennies the pounds always returned and with interest.

I decided to take matters into my own hands. I read every diet and fitness magazine from cover to cover and mapped out my own healthy eating crusade. The goal was to stick to the programme while eating healthily, feeling satisfied and enjoying what I ate. To meet this challenge I had to create the recipes myself to get me through. In time I became a wizard at the trickery and techniques of low-fat cooking. The hard work paid off; I steadily lost weight. Indian food, often the culprit for my falling off the healthy eating wagon, was my saving grace and it still keeps me firmly on track.

This is not a diet manual, just a book full of healthy and, if I do say so myself, delicious recipes to help you transform the mundane into something more tempting. These recipes changed my life and I put pen to paper in the hope that they help improve yours.

spice up your health

I know it is a cliché but I have absolutely no doubt that you are a product of how you live. I went from . . . ahem . . . generous proportions to a size ten by regulating my food intake and exercising. As a result, apart from losing weight I found myself effervescing with energy; my skin was clear, my eyes were bright, my hair shone and I looked about eight years younger. I looked and felt better than ever.

Had I spent a little time reading about India's own medical heritage I would have found out everything I needed to know. The ancient wisdom of Ayurveda (meaning knowledge of how to live) has been guiding the population of India on how to maintain optimum health for over five thousand years. Our bodies are delicately balanced systems and small external changes or stresses disturb our natural equilibrium. Ayurveda practitioners prescribe appropriate diets, natural medicines and lots of rest to cure these imbalances.

Following an Ayurvedic diet (which is an eating plan rather than systematic deprivation) means enjoying a variety of freshly cooked meals, with a balance of flavours and nutrients. Depending on your particular imbalance, the doctor may ask you to avoid sour, bitter, sweet, astringent or heavy food, raw vegetables or any food that would delay your return to health. The general rules are:

- All meals should supply the body with carbohydrates, protein and a little fat.
- Restrict meats and alcohol.
- Avoid additives and preservatives.
- Limit your intake of raw vegetables as they are considered difficult to digest.
- Stick to whole grains rather than refined products.
- Meals should be freshly prepared and hot to aid digestion.
- You should only sit down to a meal once the last one has been digested.
- The food type should suit the time of the year with more sweet and sour food being eaten in the winter (that is, more carbohydrates and fats).
- Focus on your meal as you eat, maintain an even pace and stop when you are full.
- Lastly, for all the vibration-sensitive people out there, the food should be prepared lovingly and eaten in a relaxing atmosphere.

Most of this advice will sound familiar and is good common sense. This may seem excessive, but a look at the ingredients listed on the packet of any convenience meal will show just how many things go into it. I know most of us don't have the time to think about what to eat, let alone cook it, but the positive effects of doing so will last longer than a session at the gym or an evening in the pub.

Indian meals traditionally contain a spectrum of ingredients spanning the food groups. The building blocks of Indian cuisine are now accepted as being highly beneficial for health and are revered for their preventative and curative powers. The main super-ingredients are tomatoes, onions, garlic, ginger, yoghurt and spices. In fact, spices are considered to be the *crème de la crème*, possessing powerful antibacterial and antioxidant properties. Indian sages discovered and understood these benefits centuries ago and carefully wove them into the fabric of our cuisine. Some of these healing properties are outlined in the Food Glossary (p. 216).

india's culinary quilt

With a population of around 1 billion people, a multitude of cultures and a handful of religions, India is rightfully known as a subcontinent. The country is divided into states, each with its own character, cooking and language. Regional cuisine is still based on local agriculture, climate and general topography. India's culinary quilt was then further patterned by the many invaders and settlers who called India their home. They brought with them their own culinary traditions, which were then inextricably blended with local ingredients to create new dishes and tastes. You can still see Portuguese-inspired dishes in the South-East and Persian pilaffs in the North.

We all know by now that the menu of most Indian restaurants would sound alien in one of our own Indian kitchens. If you told native Indians that you were serving them a 'jalfrezi', 'korma' or 'balti' dish, they would probably get excited at the thought of tasting something exotic. Ingenious restaurants in India have their own set of names to distinguish dishes but these too are distinct from the ones we use at home. A lot of royal words reflect the richness of a dish, such as *muglai* (royal) or *shahi* (regal). A chef has to impress his customers and could not serve them food they would eat at home.

Some of my recipes do have a few restaurant menu elements, but to me real Indian food is peasant food. Before I have everyone up in arms, yes, I know that the gourmet moguls and opulent maharajas enjoyed regal feasts every day. But they were the exception rather than the rule. There was no refrigeration then, so meals were made daily from fresh produce sold in the street. Even today in the capital city you find street vendors pushing trolleys piled high with vegetables, shouting out the names of their wares to the households they pass. Everything was seasonal, with summer meals tailored to the heat and winter meals to the cold.

Most of my dishes stem from traditional northern Indian cooking. I have also added a smattering of regional fare as well as a few dishes that came about as a result of my own experimentation, yet even these retain a strong, clear character. I don't believe people cook and serve several courses for themselves any more. Our meals are based more upon mood, situation and circumstance. I have grouped the recipes to reflect the modern-day attitude to meals and food rather than the more traditional 'by course' format. The index, grouping recipes by the main ingredient, will help you mix and match dishes from different chapters.

the meal

As the world continues to shrink, we have come to understand that there is no 'wrong' way to eat and that different cultures have their own customs and habits. Accepted wisdom ranges from 'eat three good meals a day' to 'graze your way through six small ones'. Add to this the fact that our hectic lifestyles barely allow us time for two and we can safely say that 'mealtime laws' have become hazy. I don't believe in fixed rules but there are some cultural guidelines.

Traditional Indian meals are casual affairs with everyone serving themselves from big bowls of food in the centre of the table. These dishes complement each other with regard to taste, texture, nutrition and temperature. A typical family meal could consist of a chicken dish (*dry, protein*), a lentil curry (*saucy, protein and fibre*), a seasonal vegetable (*minerals, vitamins and fibre*), yoghurt (*cooling*), salad (*texture*) and pickles or chutneys (*sweet and spicy*). This would be served with flat-bread or rice (*complex carbohydrate*). There is normally only one course and it is relished. Appetisers and desserts are saved for guests. This is low-frills, high-flavour, wholesome food.

If you don't want a traditional meal or are cooking for just the one or two of you, mix and match the recipes or pair with your normal family dishes. Serve toast instead of *roti* or toss gravied dishes with pasta. Make sandwiches with leftovers; one of my favourites is made with *Potatoes with Cauliflower* (p. 147) and grilled. Serve a roast meal with *Potatoes with Cumin Seeds* (p. 165) and *Spicy Peas* (p. 61). Dip a hunk of bread into a *Mixed Lentil Curry* (p. 141) for a light and warming lunch. Some dishes, however, are best served together, and I point this out where relevant.

Indian food is ideal for those in a hurry as most dishes actually benefit from being made in advance, allowing the flavours to mingle. Breads can be wrapped in foil and warmed in the oven; rice can be reheated, covered, in the microwave or plunged into boiling water to heat through; and most pickles and many chutneys keep for months. Even desserts are mostly made in advance and served chilled. I do prefer to make our vegetable dishes freshly but again do as you would normally.

THE KITCHEN

kitchen equipment

You probably already have most of the necessary items or you may find that you want to update your existing kitchen equipment and utensils. I use the following on a daily basis and they help to make my cooking more pleasure than pain.

I know the current advice is not to measure anything and to just use your instincts but my inner goddess has led to many burnt rice dishes, under-sauced curries and countless hungry diners. Learn from my experience and get a set of kitchen scales to measure everything until you get a good idea of approximations.

A good knife is imperative when cooking Indian food. There is a lot of chopping required and a heavy sharp knife makes light work of a potentially arduous task.

No self-respecting healthy eater would be without a set of non-stick pans, which allow food to be cooked in minimal amounts of oil. A good-quality pan will retain its coating longer so choose a reliable brand with a tight-fitting lid. Never use metal utensils with these pans as they scrape away the coating.

A tava, or shallow, concave, cast-iron pan, is used to cook most Indian breads and roast spices. A flat griddle pan or non-stick frying pan can be used instead.

Muslin, also known as cheesecloth, is a very thin material that is mostly used when making *paneer* (home-made white cheese) and draining yoghurt. It is also great for draining and squeezing out excess liquid from grated vegetables.

A large metal spoon is essential; it does a better job than wooden spoons in scraping the bottom of a pan when making *Thickened Milk* (p. 36); it will not transfer colours or flavours, unlike wooden spoons; and it is better at skimming fat or scum off the surface of liquids (though don't use it on a non-stick pan).

Tongs are indispensable for turning foods or when grilling or cooking flat-breads.

Grinders, food processors and blenders are real kitchen facilitators. Great for grinding spices, making pastes and purées, kneading, chopping and slicing. There are, of course, other ways of achieving the same effect using a pestle and mortar, a grater or a knife. For some recipes a food processor or blender is indispensable, in which case this is indicated in the recipe introduction.

Lastly a rolling pin is necessary to roll and shape Indian breads.

behind the scenes

By mealtime, I'm ready to eat the entire contents of my fridge and the last thing I want to do is run out to the shops, picking up the ingredients I need. So, having learned through experience, I now stock up on anything that cuts down my cooking time or has a long shelf-life. Luckily, the modern supermarket is a boon and is packed with convenient and exotic products. However, you will need to go to an ethnic store for some of the spices and ingredients which often are cheaper and fresher than in most local supermarkets.

The following list is a rough guide of useful store-cupboard items to stock up on.

grains and cereals

Ready-made chapattis, *naans* and chapatti flour; long-grain Basmati rice and rice flour; coarse-grain semolina; gram flour (*besan*) (a yellow flour similar to chickpea flour); frozen filo pastry.

legumes

Cans and packets of dried kidney beans, chickpeas, black-eyed peas, green peas. Also, whole, or split and skinned: Bengal gram, mung beans, red lentils, pigeon peas and black gram.

dried fruits and nuts

Golden raisins, almonds, pistachios, desiccated coconut and cashew nuts.

vegetables

Peeled and chopped canned tomatoes (canned tomatoes are not as tart as fresh ones so add a little lemon juice or yoghurt to the recipe); fresh garlic cloves, ginger and dried tamarind, chopped or made into pastes; dried or crushed red chillies (stronger than fresh ones so add sparingly); canned potatoes, canned sweetcorn; frozen spinach, peas and lotus root.

spices

Bay leaves, black cardamom pods, black peppercorns, green cardamom pods, carom seeds, chilli powder, cinnamon sticks, cloves, coriander seeds, cumin seeds, dried curry leaves, fennel seeds, dried fenugreek leaves, fenugreek seeds, blades of mace, dried mango powder, brown mustard seeds, nigella (onion) seed powder, dried pomegranate seeds, saffron strands, turmeric powder, channa masala, chaat masala, *pao bhaji masala* and *saambar* powder.

miscellaneous

Bottled lemon juice, skimmed milk (long-life) and low-fat yoghurt; tomato purée; frozen, skinless joints of meat, poultry and fillets of fish; frozen quorn chunks and mince (available in the UK); fresh eggs.

fridge and freezer

Indian dishes store and freeze really well, but make sure you follow basic principles for fridge and freezer management.

fridge Store cooked dishes covered with cling film, plus a lid or foil, to retain freshness and to stop the flavours from leaking and spreading to other foods.

Keeping lives: most cooked dishes, 1–2 days; *paneer*, 2–3 days in fresh water; milk, 2–3 days; yoghurt, about 4 days, after which it becomes more and more sour. In India, yoghurt is often soured especially for use in yoghurt curries, so if this has happened accidentally, that is one way of using it up.

freezer When freezing small items like samosas, open-freeze on a baking tray and then store in a freezer-proof container. This stops them freezing into a solid mass and makes it possible to take out only a couple at a time.

Freeze *Everyday Curry Paste* (p. 28), garlic paste and ginger paste (p. 30) in an ice-cube tray so that you can pop out small portions and use as directed.

Stuffed breads freeze well when layered between sheets of greaseproof paper.

Keeping lives are roughly as follows: unblanched raw vegetables, 1 month; milk puddings, 3 months; breads, up to 3 months; prawns, 3 months; *paneer* and ice cream, such as *kulfi*, 4 months; oily fish, 4 months; mince, 4 months; meat (lamb, poultry and game), 6 months; raw fruit, 7–8 months; white fish, 8 months; cooked fruit and blanched raw vegetables, up to 1 year.

Defrost frozen foods thoroughly overnight in the fridge for best results.

reheating Bring refrigerated food back to room temperature before reheating (allow at least 1 hour). Wrap in foil to prevent it drying out in the oven. Leave the foil open if you want a crisp finish (for example, with samosas). Use a moderate temperature – 180°C/350°F/Gas 4 – rather than a high one for previously frozen dishes and make sure they are piping hot before eating.

GETTING STARTED

AT FIRST GLANCE, Indian food seems complex enough to scare off the most seasoned cooks. This chapter should help calm these fears as it includes cooking hints, preparation tips and techniques that are used in these recipes, from roasting the spices to understanding the balance of flavours. Many tips are obvious but may help those who are new to the kitchen.

cooking hints

Please do read the following hints before you begin to cook. They will help the dishes to come out as they should.

Read the recipe first to ensure that you have all the necessary equipment and ingredients. Then measure and prepare the ingredients so that once you start cooking, you won't have to run around the kitchen at the wrong time. On the other hand you may be a seasoned cook and know how to organise yourself so that you can chop while the meal is cooking.

Cooking is not a science and the exact cooking time varies with the freshness, size and origin of the ingredients. Also, ingredients behave differently each time you use them. For example, a tomato can be sweet or tart, flavourful or watery. So you may need to add a squeeze of lemon juice for the right level of sharpness. The same rules apply to all fresh produce. The only way to know your ingredient is to taste it and adjust the accompanying flavour accordingly. Likewise, you may need to add extra water when cooking vegetables or pulses as they respectively release or absorb different amounts of liquid.

I find gas cookers easier to control and hotter than electric cookers, so if you use the latter add a little extra cooking time to those indicated. These are guidelines only; follow the descriptions of how the dish should look and smell at the different stages.

Until recently, there were no ovens in India. In fact, most households wouldn't know what to do with one even today. The nearest equivalent would be the *tandoor*, a barrel-shaped oven, which reaches mercurial temperatures, cooking anything inside in record time. These days, however, the oven can be a godsend for busy

people, where you can leave meat or vegetables to take care of themselves until dinnertime. A few oven-cooked recipes are included, but if you prefer you can cook any of the curry dishes in the oven once the basic gravy has been made.

Taste is as individual as people so if you are an Indian food novice adjust the levels of chilli, garlic and spice accordingly. Batches of spices and chillies also differ in potency so do not be too heavy-handed. I have sweetened the desserts to my own taste, which is a little mean compared to traditional Indian tastes, so add more sugar if you like your desserts particularly sweet. Or use fructose, a natural fruit sugar, which is sweeter than sugar so you don't need to add as much.

Many people are tempted to pick up jars of powdered spices from the supermarket spice rack. This would be a real shame as whole seeds are now easily available and, when freshly ground, impart a far superior flavour and aroma to food. Most whole spices (cinnamon is an exception) keep well in airtight containers and take minutes to grind (see p. 21).

My most precious kitchen possession is my spice box. I grind small quantities of spices and decant them into individual small circular containers, which reside in the box. When I cook, I have all these spices handy without my workspace being too cluttered. If you cannot face grinding your own spices, you may need to add a little more of each spice for the same intensity of flavour. Keep tasting and you will be fine.

The cow is a sacred animal in Hinduism, the predominant religion of India, so beef is rarely eaten. However, the recipes can be adapted to suit your eating preferences. Substitute like ingredients with like; for example, change lamb for beef.

Coriander is much more than a garnish. It has a definite flavour that brings Indian food to life. I always stir a handful into the pan just before taking it off the heat. Bundles of fresh coriander are cheaper from Indian shops. Store by washing, drying and chopping the herb, then sealing in a plastic bag to refrigerate or freeze. Use straight from the freezer as it will thaw in the saucepan.

Many recipes call for the gravy to be reduced. Extra water is often added to a dish at various stages to help it cook. This excess liquid can then be boiled off.

In India, dishes are often prepared in advance and then reheated at mealtimes. If cooked dishes are waiting, and therefore cooling, the gravy or sauce will continue to thicken and a little extra liquid will have to be added.

key flavours

The basic make-up of Indian dishes is a harmonious combination of mild and strong spices, savoury ingredients, a degree of tartness and, sometimes, a hint of sweetness. The following will give you a better understanding of the different flavours and the way I use them.

souring agents

A sour element is essential in Indian dishes. Often a dish will taste no more than average until the flavours are perked up with the addition of something tart such as a squeeze of lemon juice. The other sources of tartness we use are tomatoes, yoghurt, tamarind and dried mango powder.

Generally speaking, these ingredients are interchangeable as they all add the required tartness. However, each also imparts its own unique character to a dish. Tomatoes add a rich colour and flavour while yoghurt adds creaminess. Dried mango powder has a pleasing, subtle, fruity tang, as does tamarind. Lemon juice is the ultimate, no-frills souring agent. Try to use the suggested ingredient; otherwise substitute one of the others.

butter, oil or ghee

I use good-quality safflower oil, high in polyunsaturated fats, for nearly everything. It doesn't interfere with the flavours and doesn't burn at high temperatures. At times I use mustard oil, when I need a stronger flavour.

Ghee, synonymous with Indian cooking, is butter that has been cleared of impure solids, leaving a clean, liquid butter or a semi-solid mass. There have been many debates as to the benefits and hazards of butter or oil as well as the health benefits of ghee (an Ayurvedic argument). I will only say that all three conduct and enhance flavour, and have a similar fat and calorie content. It is said that ghee should last for ever without turning rancid, and in fact the medicinal properties of ghee are said to improve with age. Use whichever fat you prefer in moderation, choosing oil for cooking and butter for adding smoothness and flavour.

salt and spice and all things nice . . .

Spices are the foundation of Indian food. They may be used raw and ground, dry-roasted, or cooked in fat. In essence, the three methods are not interchangeable as each treatment imparts a different flavour. Buying whole spices allows you access to a greater range of flavours.

From single spices to the spice mix, the most popular of which is garam masala. Literally translated as 'hot spices', this is one of the main components of North Indian food. There is no exact recipe as it varies from one house to the next. Ready-made varieties often contain too much of the cheaper cumin and coriander seeds and less of the other aromatics. Grinding your own blend takes just minutes and it will be far more powerful in flavour as well as cheaper than bought varieties. Indian shops sell packs of the whole spices that go into a standard garam masala. For my traditional garam masala recipe see p. 31. If you do use a ready-made version you may need to add a little extra for the same intensity of flavour.

There are some exceptions. All Indians use certain ready-prepared spice mixes, blended for specific dishes or ingredients. One of the most popular is *channa masala*, which adds flavour to any chickpea dish. Another popular one is *chaat masala*. This spicy, salty blend is sprinkled over barbecued foods and snacks and will be found in most Indian kitchens. I cannot leave out two of my favourites. *Saambar* powder is used when making the famous *Vegetable and Lentil Curry* (see p. 144). The other, *pao bhaji masala*, is used when making the spicy roadside snack of this name. These spice blends are one of our culinary secrets and really do add extra layers of complexity to a dish.

We have quite a heavy hand when it comes to seasoning. Indian food does need a generous amount of salt to balance the robust spices. As a guide, I add one teaspoon of salt to a dish for four people. Black salt (or *kala namak*) also deserves a mention. This pungent, dirty grey salt has a natural spicy flavour and, used sparingly, it does add an extra dimension to a dish.

Dried pomegranate powder is made from pomegranate seeds, roasted for 1–2 minutes and then ground. The seeds are hard and somewhat sticky so can be difficult to grind; use the powder if available.

red-hot chilli peppers

Chillies are such an integral part of Indian food that outsiders believe all dishes are rampant with this popular spice. Yes, we do love our chillies. They add more than a kick; they bring a dish to life. Many Indians find a meal without chilli tasteless, regardless of the other flavours. It is like salt to many of us. That said, I know a lot of Indians who don't eat any chillies at all, so they are not essential. It would, however, be a shame to miss out on their wonderful flavour in avoiding their heat. I often add green chillies whole, so that they impart their savour without exposing the real culprits, the seeds and inner membranes. The chilli should not bully the other flavours unless it is a chilli-flavoured dish; instead it should combine with the other spices to give life to any ingredient. It is all about balance.

As with bell peppers or capsicums, green chillies become red as they ripen. Both are equally hot but do have slightly different flavours. I find the flavour of red chillies sweeter and more rounded but each has its own place. Indians use the fresh, long, slim chillies as well as the tiny and devilishly hot dried red ones. They may seem shrivelled specimens of their former glory, but don't be fooled by their insubstantial appearance: these babies really pack a punch. Crumble them or add whole to a dish for a flavoured heat. An ideal store-cupboard favourite. If you are unable to find them, keep a jar of crushed chilli flakes and add to taste. Red chilli powder is used in all Indian homes; although it is very colourful and quite hot, it lacks something in comparison.

onions

Onions take different lengths of time to cook, depending on how finely you chop them, the quantity you cook, the amount of oil you use and the level of heat. The less oil you use, the more slowly onions cook and the more careful you have to be as they burn more easily. It is often better to err on the side of too much oil, rather than not enough.

When cooking a small amount, use a moderate heat, which will cook the onions to golden in 5–6 minutes. If cooking a whole medium chopped onion until golden, use a low heat, which will take around 15 minutes.

I use onions in three stages: soft (when they have turned translucent), golden (when they have shrivelled up a little) and brown. One has to be careful when taking them to the last level, so I add a splash of water to make sure they do not burn.

preparation and recipe tips

For the best results, cook rice, pulses and meats over a low heat. *Always* use the best-quality and freshest ingredients you can. Meals cooked and taken when you are relaxed also taste a lot better than those snatched on the move.

removing the flesh from a mango

Mangoes contain a large, flat, rugby-ball-shaped stone in their centre. To remove the flesh, stand the fruit upright with the thinner edge towards you. Visualise the stone in the middle of the mango and, using a sharp knife, make vertical slits in the plump cheeks on either side of the stone. Cut lengthways into two long wedges. Then cut the remaining wedges from the other sides. You can easily peel off the skins with your hands or scrape away with a spoon.

skinning tomatoes

Plunge tomatoes into boiling water for 45 seconds. Use a sharp knife to make a slit in the skin and gently peel it off. I often cheat and grate my tomatoes. This purées the tomato and leaves the skin in your hand; it takes just seconds. Where the recipe calls for ground tomatoes you can skin and purée them or grate them. It is up to you.

adding water

Apparently, adding cold water to a hot dish can impair its flavour. I haven't done the taste test but go with accepted wisdom on this. Water must always be heated and not used straight from the cold tap. I always put the kettle on before I start cooking and use this boiled, still-hot water so that I don't have to keep bringing the pan contents to the boil before continuing.

grinding and roasting spices

Spices are roasted for two reasons: first to facilitate the grinding of potentially soggy seeds (India can be very damp) and secondly to change the basic flavour. For example, cumin seeds are used whole as they are sold, roasted or ground. In England, you would not need to roast these seeds to grind them but during the monsoons in India, the damp gets into everything and the seeds would need a light roasting to crisp them up enough to grind them but not to change the flavour. When you roast for flavour (this is always indicated in the ingredients list) roast until the spice releases an aroma and turns a shade or two darker.

To roast spices, use a flat Indian cast-iron pan (*tava*) or frying pan. Ideally dry-roast spices individually as they take different lengths of time to cook. Roast over a low to moderate heat, shaking the pan often to help them brown evenly. Be careful as they burn in the blink of an eye. They are roasted once they are fragrant, around 1–2 minutes.

Grind spices in a small coffee mill (which is obviously solely dedicated to spice-grinding activities) or use a sturdy pestle and mortar.

We use roasted cumin powder in a lot of our chutneys and yoghurt dishes. It does not need to be cooked further. Roast whole cumin seeds for 1 minute and then grind.

dried beans and pulses

Pulses is the collective term used for beans, lentils and peas.

First, check that there are no stones or grit in your pulses. Wash in several changes of clean water until the water runs clear. Dried beans (but not lentils) must be soaked overnight or for at least 8 hours to render them more digestible. Simply cover the beans with plenty of water. The following morning, the soaking water should be discarded.

Once they have been soaked, cook pulses in a large saucepan, covered by at least 5cm (2 inches) of fresh water. Cooking times will depend very much on how old the beans are. Chickpeas should be brought to the boil, covered and simmered until tender, about 60 minutes. Kidney beans should be boiled rapidly for 10 minutes, then simmered for a further 45 minutes or until tender.

It is often said that salt should not be added when cooking pulses as it makes them tough. However, most Indians cook pulses with salt and are known for their lentil and bean curries. If you are unsure, add salt at the end of cooking. That said, you should always add a pinch of bicarbonate of soda to the water in which you cook any dried bean, which keeps them soft.

One thing to remember is that lentils hate to be hurried: for the best results, cook over the lowest heat.

quick-soak method If you forget to soak the beans beforehand, follow this quick-soak method. Place the dried beans in a large saucepan and cover with plenty of water. Bring to the boil and simmer for 8–10 minutes. Remove from the heat and leave to soak in the cooking liquor for 3 hours. Drain. Fill the pan with fresh water. Bring to the boil again and simmer until the beans are tender.

sprouting Dried mung beans can be sprouted to make bean sprouts. Soak overnight in plenty of cold water. The following morning, drain and wrap the wet beans in cheesecloth or muslin. Leave for another night in a dark place. The beans should sprout by the following morning. If not, dampen the cloth again and leave until they do. Boil the sprouts in fresh salted water for about 15–20 minutes on a medium heat until tender but al dente. Drain and cool and use as directed.

cooking and preparing meat and fish

Indian poultry are smaller and scrawnier than their Western cousins. Although we never bone them, we always skin them. This allows the flavours to penetrate well into the flesh. We normally buy whole chickens and joint them at home. Members of the family then help themselves to their favourite parts. The leg and thigh joints are moist and have more flavour than the leaner breast, with the wings being the fattiest of them all. We eat with our fingers and chew on the soft and succulent bones to extract as much flavour and pleasure as possible. To save on time and effort, my regular butcher hands me bags of jointed and skinned chicken, which I just rinse when I get home and cook or freeze for later use.

When cooking chicken it is important to remember that all the joints should be of a similar size so that they all cook in the same amount of time. If anything, cut the breast pieces slightly larger than the other joints as they cook more quickly. When using larger birds, cut the breast into three pieces and the thighs and drumsticks in half. The actual cooking time depends on the size of the bird, the individual pieces and the cooking temperature. You can stew chicken over a very low heat for 1 hour but it also stir-fries in minutes.

Chicken is cooked when the flesh springs back when pressed. Alternatively, insert the tip of a knife into the thickest part of the joint, press down on the meat and, if the juices run clear, it is cooked. If in doubt test it with a meat thermometer. Poultry is cooked when its internal temperature reaches 180°C (350°F). Cooked chicken flesh should be clear of any pink tint.

I find that leg and shoulder cuts of lamb are ideal for slow cooking in curries or stews. As a bonus, they are cheaper than some of the other cuts, which are better suited to plain grilling. When I buy lamb chops, I spend a few minutes trimming off the excess fat. When in season, I opt for spring lamb, which although more expensive than the usual lamb, far surpasses it with its delicate flavour and meat.

Lamb is cooked when it is tender and springs back to the touch. Indians normally cook meat until it has no pink in the middle and is meltingly tender, practically falling off the bone. If in doubt, test with a meat thermometer. Ground red meat should be cooked to 160°C (320°F) while whole cuts are cooked when they reach 165°C (330°F). Reheat meat dishes to an internal temperature of 165°C (330°F).

Northern fish dishes are normally made with firm-fleshed freshwater fish whereas southern and north-eastern parts are blessed with a treasure chest of options, having the sea at their doorstep. You can use any fish you like as long as it is a robust type that will not disintegrate into the sauce. When buying fish, choose those that smell of the sea rather than, well, fish. When buying whole fish, look for bright eyes and shiny skin, which indicate freshness. You can leave the bone in or remove it, but keeping the bone in helps the fish retain its shape. Fish is cooked when it turns opaque.

To prepare prawns, remove the shell, cut a thin, shallow slit along the back and remove the thin black vein. Rinse and pat dry. Cook just before serving as reheated or overcooked prawns become tough. This takes just minutes. Once cooked, the prawns will have curled up and turned a peachy-pink colour.

Marinating ensures that flavours will permeate meat right the way through while tenderising it at the same time. Without doubt, this process enhances the taste and texture of the dish. I marinate most delicate-textured fish and seafood for about 30 minutes; any longer and the flesh fibres can break down too much, making the fish mushy. Fish with a denser texture can be marinated for much longer, as can prawns. The recipes in this book use firm-textured fish and marinades that are not too acidic. Poultry and lamb can be marinated for 24 hours, if not longer, but once you pass the 1-hour mark you should cover the meat and leave it in the fridge. Remove 1 hour before cooking to bring it back to room temperature.

through thick and thin

You don't need fat for thick sauces. Add one of the following key ingredients for extra body.

Coriander powder was a favourite choice in my mother's family. They never ate onions and used this spice to thicken and flavour their curries. Add judiciously and keep tasting as it is quite aromatic.

Use vegetable or bean purées. When cooking a dish with these ingredients, remove a small amount of the vegetables or beans and blend or process, stirring back in for gravy with body.

Yoghurt will thicken and enrich a dish. Add to taste; too much can make a dish sour, disturbing the balance of flavours.

Even though rice flour is not a traditional thickening agent, I often add a spoonful (dissolved in water) to thin gravy. The added bonus is a coconut-like flavour.

Indians often add gram flour (*besan*) or maize flour to a dish to help bind it or thicken the gravy. Cook after adding, stirring, for 2–3 minutes.

For coconut flavour there is nothing like the real thing – well, nearly the real thing. Coconut milk powder is my new favourite coconut ingredient, replacing coconut cream and coconut milk. It can provide just the right degree of coconut flavour to any dish, magically giving it the taste of southern India. Again, it is rich so don't be too heavy handed.

If your gravy lacks colour as well as body, try tomato purée or even some canned plum tomatoes, cooking well to reduce the excess liquid. Other colour-donors are turmeric and paprika, but add only a little as they can change the flavours of a dish.

And if you want a touch of richness and smoothness, add a final, small knob of butter.

pickles

The secret to a lasting pickle is an absence of moisture in the vegetables and normally a lot of mustard oil. Some well-made pickles last for years. In India the searing heat will dry vegetables left in the sun in a single day. In the UK, with the damp air and lack of sun, it takes a lot longer (if ever). One way to ensure an absence of moisture is to steam the vegetables, dry them thoroughly in a clean tea towel and dry them overnight in a warm place or oven.

Pickles are always made with mustard oil. If you use a milder vegetable oil, you will end up with a milder pickle, lacking the depth of flavour expected. I have reduced the amount of oil used, however, and as a consequence some of the pickles in this book will not last more than a month, after which mould begins to form. But I feel this is worth the saving in fat. Store pickles in sterilised jars in a dry and dark place.

To sterilise jars, wash them thoroughly with soapy water. Place in a preheated oven for 4–5 minutes so that they dry out completely. Fill and seal, using meticulously clean hands and utensils. As with jam, once you break the seal always use a clean, dry spoon to avoid introducing impurities into the jar.

Pickles must be shaken regularly a few times every day for the first 5–7 days for the flavours to develop. If possible, leave them in the sun for as long as you can every day while they are maturing. To check whether they are ready either smell them or taste them – you can't tell just by looking. The pickle should be tart, with rounded flavours.

BASIC RECIPES

A CUISINE OFTEN has a handful of defining ingredients and key recipes that form its building blocks. A delve into any country's food will highlight these, often close-guarded, treasures: rich stock, creamy white sauce, fragrant bouquets garnis, expertly balanced tomato sauce, perfect pastry, ethnic spice blends or the secret family recipe for garam masala. Experimenting with any new food can be daunting, so getting to grips with the basics will make the difference between a good try and an authentic dish.

I know you can buy everything in the shops these days but nothing beats home-made food and that includes the basics: bread, cheese and live yoghurt. And as these recipes are easy, as well as being cheaper and healthier than store-bought items, there doesn't seem to be any competition. So get cooking.

PASS THE PASTE

Pastes are really easy to knock up and they create smooth sauces with homogenous flavours. Also, they can be prepared in advance, and used as and when needed. These are a few of the key pastes used in Indian cooking.

tamarind paste
IMLI KA PASTE

Tamarind is sold in dried blocks, as a paste and as a concentrate. I always choose the block form as it keeps well and I feel I have more control over the ingredient. The paste, used judiciously, works just as well but I suggest that you avoid the concentrate as it is very powerful and can easily ruin a dish.

To extract the juice from the tamarind, cut 2.5–5cm (1–2 inches) off the block and cover with 4cm (1½ inches) of hot water. Leave for 15–20 minutes to soften. Using a fork, mash the softened pulp into the water. Squeeze the solids to extract all the juice and discard together with the pods, or pass through a sieve. If you wish, you can make a paste from the whole block and store it in an ice-cube tray in the freezer where it will keep for several months.

everyday curry paste
ROZ MARRA KI MASALA

This curry paste has vastly improved my kitchen life and is one of the most versatile and useful products in my fridge. It is the soul of a curry and once you have a jar on hand, Indian cooking becomes simplicity itself. It does take up to 1 hour to make but it lasts for around 2 weeks in the fridge. Alternatively, freeze into tablespoon-size portions in an ice-cube tray, transfer to a plastic bag and use straight from frozen.

This paste has so many uses. Stir a spoonful into yoghurt with grated cucumber and coriander for instant *raita*. Stir into eggs for a spiced scramble. Make a spicy dip: dissolve a tablespoonful in a little milk, add a handful of chopped spring onions and thicken with low-fat cream cheese. Stir into tomato sauce or shop-bought Bolognese sauce for a spiced pasta sauce. Stir into plain rice together with a few cooked vegetables for instant pilaff. You can even add some to a bread mix for an unusual flavour. I could go on but I think you get the idea. Once you start using this paste you too will never want to be without it.

Don't cut corners with the cooking time and follow the tips for rich, deep gravy (p. 25). One of the biggest challenges is to cook the onions properly without burning them. Use a non-stick pan, cook on a low to moderate heat and stir often. Getting this paste right is important and is very much worth the effort. If you like spicy food, you can increase the quantity of spices that the recipe stipulates.

3 tbs vegetable oil

400g/14 oz onions (about 2–3 medium), finely chopped or ground

1½ tbs ginger paste

2 heaped tbs garlic paste

1–3 green chillies, left whole, or ½–1 tsp red chilli powder

1½ tsp salt

1 scant tsp turmeric powder

1½–2 tbs coriander powder

500g/1 lb 2 oz tomatoes (about 4–5 medium), grated

2 tsp tomato purée

250ml (9 fl oz) hot water

¼–½ tsp coarsely ground black pepper

1 tsp garam masala

1 level tsp cumin powder

Makes 8 good tablespoons

Heat the oil in a medium non-stick saucepan. Add the onions and fry until they start to colour. Turn the heat down, add a pinch of salt and cook, stirring, until they are a golden-brown, a further 20 minutes or so. Add splashes of water from the kettle, whenever the pan seems too dry. Reduce to cook off excess water.

Keeping the heat down, add the ginger and garlic pastes and the chillies, and cook for 30–40 seconds. Add the salt, turmeric and coriander and stir. Follow with the tomatoes and tomato purée. Turn the heat up, add the water and cook for 25 minutes, adding more water from the kettle if necessary, to prevent the pan from becoming dry. Allow the purée to reduce so that by the end it is a thick paste.

Uncover the pan and reduce the contents to a thick purée, stirring often.

Stir in the black pepper, garam masala and cumin powder. Cool and store in a sterilised jar or container in the fridge or freeze in tablespoon-sized portions in an ice-cube tray.

instant garlic and ginger pastes
LASAN AUR ADRAK KE PASTE

You can buy these, but they are easy, quick and cheap to make at home.

The quickest way of making small quantities of ginger or garlic paste is to grate peeled garlic cloves or chunks of fresh ginger. Three small garlic cloves or 2.5cm (1 inch) of peeled ginger makes 1 teaspoon of paste. To make a tablespoon of paste, you will need 5–6 large cloves of garlic or 5cm (2 inches) of peeled fresh ginger. For larger quantities, process with a tablespoon of water in a grinder or food processor. Store in an airtight container or an ice-cube tray. The pastes will keep for 2–3 days in the refrigerator or 3–4 weeks in the freezer.

Many chefs use the flat edge of a large knife to crush a garlic clove with a sprinkling of salt, which acts as an abrasive. Press down on the clove and drag the blade towards you while smearing the garlic on the salt. The salt breaks down the fibres and soon you have a paste. This technique takes a little practice but gets easier with time.

indian spice mix
GARAM MASALA

This is India's most famous and common spice blend. There is no exact recipe; each family has its own and purists would never add all the ingredients that we do in the West. Traditional garam masala is much stronger than we are used to and is added to a dish in very small quantities. Some people roast the spices; others do not. In India moisture tends to get into everything so spices have to be roasted a little to make them easy to grind. In my extended family, however, we use them unroasted. I will leave it up to you.

This is my family recipe, which I have lightened with regard to the hotter spices and replaced with milder ones. Store-bought blends of garam masala are still an option but do not compare in taste to that made at home.

Makes 10g/4 tablespoons

1 tbs cumin seeds
½ tsp black peppercorns
2 whole brown cardamom pods
2.5cm (1 inch) cinnamon stick
  or ½ tsp cinnamon powder

1 tbs coriander seeds
10 small cloves
2 bay leaves

Simply grind all the ingredients together to a fine powder. If roasting first, add to a hot pan, turn the heat down and cook, shaking the pan often. Once fragrant (which takes 1–2 minutes), remove from the pan, cool and grind. Store away from direct sunlight.

EVERYDAY GRAINS

Rice is the most widely consumed food in the world and is a staple in households all over the East. It is packed with essential nutrients and is a healthy source of complex carbohydrate. Indians use this magical grain whole, flaked, beaten and ground, and it can be found in any course at any time of the day. In the Western world, rice is gaining popularity as more of us look beyond gluten-packed wheat for a carbohydrate option. As a bonus, it is a great foil for most flavours and is so simple to cook.

rice

BASMATI

In the north, we prefer long-grained white rice and, if possible, we use Basmati. This fragrant rice grows in the foothills of the Himalayas and although it is dearer than other varieties its delicate flavour and grains are perfect with our spices. In the south, you often find the shorter, more robust, coarser grains that are grown locally. Use whichever you prefer or whatever you have at home.

preparation

Check that there is no grit among the grains. Then wash in several changes of clean water to remove any excess starch flour that may coat them. Once the water runs clear, soak the rice in fresh water for about 30 minutes. This helps elongate the grains but it is not absolutely necessary.

If you have not had the time to soak the rice, and let's face it life is like that, just measure the rice by volume, wash under cold running water, put straight into the saucepan and top with twice the same volume of water. Bring to the boil, then turn the heat down as low as possible, cover and cook undisturbed for 14–15 minutes. Alternatively, cook by the boiling method, see below, for 10 minutes.

cooking

You can cook rice in a heavy-based saucepan, non-stick pan or ovenproof casserole. The pan must have a tight-fitting lid if you are using the absorption method (see below). An average portion of boiled rice is 30–50g (1–1¾ oz) per person, depending on the eater. There are two ways to cook plain rice.

the absorption method By volume I use 1 measure of soaked rice to just under 1½ measures of water. So for 100g (3½ oz) rice or 125ml (4½ fl oz), I use 180ml (6 fl oz) water. Bring the water to the boil, add salt to taste and stir in the soaked rice. Bring back to the boil, then cover tightly, reduce the heat to its lowest setting and cook, undisturbed, for about 10–12 minutes until the grain is just tender. Take off the heat and leave undisturbed to steam, covered, for 10 minutes. Then uncover and fluff up with a fork, allowing the rice to dry off a little.

the boiling method Add the soaked rice to plenty of boiling salted water. Bring back to the boil and cook undisturbed over a moderate heat for about 5–6 minutes (10 minutes for unsoaked rice) until the grain is tender. Check by squeezing a grain between your finger and thumb. There should be no thin white line in the middle but the grain should not be mushy. I often take the rice off the heat when there is still a white line in the middle and then let it steam to perfection. To do this, drain the rice into a colander placed over the still-hot pan, off the heat. Cover and leave undisturbed for 10 minutes.

rustic flat-bread
ROTI

This is India's most popular bread, and is eaten with practically every meal in the North. These small round breads are made with a mixture of plain and wholewheat flour and can be flat or puffed, small or large, fat or thin, according to region. Making the dough is easy and kneading can be quite therapeutic. It doesn't matter if they're not exactly circular and, anyway, rustic is in. Chapatti flour is a blend of flours and is sold in most large supermarkets, but if you can't find any use equal quantities of wholewheat and plain flour. You can make the dough earlier in the day and leave it in the fridge, covered with a damp cloth. Bring it back to room temperature and knead for 1 further minute before starting. You can also cook flat-breads in advance and reheat them in the oven wrapped in foil.

Makes 4 small *rotis* (quantities can be halved or doubled)

100g (3½ oz) chapatti flour or half wholewheat and half plain flour, plus extra for rolling
salt (optional)

around 50–60ml (2–2½ fl oz) cold water
2 tsp vegetable oil (optional)

Mix the flour with the salt (if using) in a bowl. Drizzle over most of the wet ingredients and get stuck in with your hands. You may not need all the water as flour absorbs different amounts, depending on its age and the moisture content in the air.

Knead for 6–7 minutes as you would any dough, adding extra water if necessary, until it comes together. The finished dough should spring back at a touch and be easy to roll out. If you have the time, leave it to rest for 30 minutes, covered, in a warm place. (This produces softer bread.)

Divide the dough into 4 equal portions and, using your hands, roll firmly into tight balls. Keep one and cover the rest. Flatten slightly and dip each side into a bowl of your flour, enough to stop it sticking while rolling. Roll out into thin, 12cm (5 inch) circles. The easiest way is to keep rotating the dough as you roll.

Heat a *tava* or non-stick frying pan until very hot. Toss the chapatti from one hand to the other to remove any excess flour (otherwise it will burn while cooking and turn the bread yellow) and place on the *tava* or in the frying pan. Cook until it is golden, and small blisters appear on the underside, about 30 seconds, then turn over. It should not stick to the pan. Keep checking the underside and when little brown spots start to appear, turn over again. This stage takes only 1½–2 minutes.

Many people like their *roti* to be puffed. There are two ways to do this. If you have a gas hob, use a pair of tongs and carefully place the bread on the open flame after it is cooked. Keep turning over the bread. Once the bread puffs up it is done. This takes a maximum of about 10 seconds. Alternatively, leave the *roti* in the pan, take a clean tea towel and gently press on different areas of the roti. The other areas should puff up.

Keep the bread warm by wrapping in cloth or foil and put in a warm oven until needed. Repeat with the remaining dough.

MILK AND YOGHURT

Dairy products such as milk and yoghurt play an important part in Indian cookery and yoghurt, especially, is used to calm the fieriness of many spicy dishes.

thickened milk
GHARA DOODH

Thickened milk is a base in many Indian puddings. It is thinner and lighter than cream, which used to be a luxury and, therefore, very expensive. Use as stated in the recipes or create your own dishes by infusing it with spices, and using it to soak dried fruits or to braise sweet vegetables or grains. It makes great breakfast muesli. If you are lactose intolerant, thicken soya milk over a very low heat. It tastes wonderful.

**1.2 litres (2 pints) semi-skimmed milk
  or soya milk**

Bring the milk to the boil in a heavy-based saucepan. Boil for 1 minute. Turn the heat down to its lowest setting and reduce by half, stirring and scraping the base of the pan with a metal spoon to prevent the milk from catching the bottom and burning. Soya milk in particular is very delicate and needs real attention when reducing, but gives excellent results. This can take from 45–60 minutes, depending on how high the heat is. The resulting milk should be a light buttery colour and have the consistency of single cream. Cool and chill.

alive and kicking yoghurt
DAHI

Yoghurt has been valued for its nutritional properties for thousands of years. It's high in protein, is a great provider of essential minerals and is full of beneficial bacteria that help to maintain a healthy gut and stomach. It also adds a certain richness and tartness to food and is great for marinating meat and chicken. Indians take advantage of this wonder food by using it in practically everything.

Many people who are lactose intolerant are able to digest plain, fresh yoghurt as it contains its own digestive enzymes. But if you prefer, you can follow this recipe using goat milk or buffalo milk. There are also many brands of soya milk yoghurt on the market.

The first time you make a yoghurt, you will require 1–2 tablespoons of live, shop-bought yoghurt to introduce the bacteria culture into the milk. For the following batch, use 1–2 tablespoons from your existing yoghurt to add to the milk. Each subsequent batch will get better and better.

Serves 4-6   **1.2 litres (2 pints) semi-skimmed milk**   **2 tbs low-fat live yoghurt, beaten**

Preheat the oven to 160°C/310°F/Gas 2½ and then turn it off. Bring the milk to the boil in a heavy-based saucepan. As soon as it starts to rise, take off the heat and cool until just warm to the touch. Stir in the yoghurt.

Pour into a glass or ceramic bowl. Cover with a plate and wrap in a tea towel. Leave to set, undisturbed, in the oven (or a warm area away from draughts), for about 5–6 hours. Refrigerate. It should stay fresh for 4–5 days.

snow-white cheese
PANEER

Paneer is home-made, unsalted, white cheese. It has a fresh flavour and a dense, crumbly texture that is a perfect foil for India's spicy flavours. It is full of virtues: it is a great source of protein, is packed with vitamins and minerals and is so moreish that even hardened carnivores find it hard to pass up a well-made *paneer* dish. Indian versions are softer and richer as they use buffalo milk, which is creamier than cow's milk and restaurants normally add cream to enrich theirs.

These days, you can buy ready-made *paneer* from the chilled section of many supermarkets but home-made *paneer* is deceptively easy to make and cheaper. I use yoghurt to curdle the milk as it produces a softer curd but you can also use lemon juice. Use any milk you like. The more fat in the milk, the softer the cheese and the more cheese you will get from the same amount of milk. Some people add salt, although I prefer the bland and fresh taste as a contrast to the spices that it is usually cooked with. A very good alternative to *paneer* is firm tofu, which is readily available in supermarkets.

Makes 125g (4 oz), enough for 2–3 when used in a dish (quantities can be doubled)

1.2 litres (2 pints) milk

100g (3½ oz) low-fat yoghurt or
    2 tbs lemon juice

salt (optional)

Bring the milk to the boil in a heavy-based saucepan. Once it starts to boil and rise up, stir in the yoghurt or lemon juice and salt if using.

Stir gently and it will soon start to curdle and separate. The curds will coagulate and the whey will be clear and slightly green. If it remains murky add another tablespoonful of yoghurt or teaspoonful of lemon juice and keep stirring. Remove from the heat.

Line a large sieve with muslin or cheesecloth and place over a large saucepan. Pour in the cheese and strain for 10 minutes. Wrap the cheese in the cloth and place a heavy weight on top, such as a water-filled saucepan, for 20–30 minutes. The cheese will flatten and form a block. Then cut into cubes or crumble, depending on how you want to use it.

Store, covered, in the refrigerator in water. You can also freeze *paneer* in an airtight container. Defrost thoroughly before use.

Paneer does not have to be cooked. It can be added to the dish at this stage. Alternatively it can be deep fried or baked for a soft interior, although this will make it dry out more quickly. Preheat the oven to 180°C/350°F/Gas 4, and bake on an oiled baking tray, drizzled with 1 scant teaspoon of oil, until just golden at the edges, about 10 minutes.

I LOVE TO graze, although this term, rather unflatteringly, comes from the eating habits of cattle. The point here is that the animals eat little and often.

There are many advantages to grazing. After every meal, as the body works to digest the food, the metabolism is raised. Eating *frequently* raises the metabolism more often, so that the body burns more calories at a constant rate. It also ensures a stable level of glucose in the blood, giving us constant energy throughout the day. When we overeat, the surge in our blood sugar levels triggers the release of an equally large dose of insulin to regulate the sugar. It is believed that elevated levels of insulin promote fat storage and reduce fat burning. Small, regular meals should help maintain even levels of insulin in the body.

THE LAZY **GRAZER**

Also, our systems often find it difficult to digest large meals at one go and we end up feeling heavy, tired and bloated. Eating smaller meals allows us to feel lighter and more alert throughout the day. Lastly (and this may just apply to me), knowing that we can eat again in a few hours stops us from overeating. I used to skip breakfast and grab something light for lunch. At dinnertime, I would eat loads of (healthy-ish) food because I was so hungry, and also because I knew that I would not eat properly for another 24 hours. This gave me a green light to have just one more bite, and then just one more. I never lost weight this way. I am now more in touch with my body and real hunger.

A word of caution! A daily regime of five small meals or snacks requires discipline. You cannot tuck into five three-course meals, all in the name of health. If you find it hard to be disciplined, stick with three good meals a day. Obviously, none of us is about to put our life on hold while we prepare and cook five meals a day. The trick is to eat a few small meals plus a snack or two in between. This chapter is full of recipes for meals for one that are quick and easy, many of which can be made in advance and are ideal packed lunches.

This sandwich is practically a national snack and can be found on menus all over India, especially at airports and railway stations. It may seem very simple but it works brilliantly. Some people toast the bread but I leave it plain so the chutney melts into the bread and keeps it really moist. Many Indians will dip the edge in a chilli sauce or ketchup.

ctc (cucumber, tomato and chutney) sandwich

TAMATAR, KHEERA AUR CHUTRI KI SANDWICHE

Serves 1

2 slices of white bread
1 rounded tsp butter, margarine or
  low-fat spread
2 rounded tsp *Green Chutney* (p. 184)

1 tomato, sliced
5–6 thin slices of cucumber
salt and freshly ground black pepper
  to taste

Spread one slice of bread with the butter and the other with the chutney. Season well. Lay the vegetables on one slice and cover with the other, cut in half and enjoy. For the perfect moist sandwich, leave it for 10 minutes so that the flavours come together.

vitality bean salad
MOONTH KA SALADE

Sprouting transforms an inert food into a live one, so sprouts are highly nutritious as well as easy to digest and absorb. This refreshing, super-healthy dish is a medley of earthy and fresh flavours and has a multitude of textures. It is great as a snack or side salad, or can be stuffed into pitta bread for a light lunch. I like to sprout my own mung beans (see p. 23 for directions), but as this needs a bit of forethought you may want to buy them already sprouted. Look for them in good supermarkets or health food shops.

Serves 1 generously (quantities can be doubled)

150g (5 oz) mung bean sprouts, rinsed, or 60g (2 oz) dried mung beans (*sabut moong dal*), sprouted
2 tbs each chopped tomato, cucumber, onion and cooked potato
½ green chilli, seeded and chopped
3 tbs finely chopped fresh coriander (leaves and stalks)

½ tsp roasted cumin powder
1 good pinch of dried mango powder
salt to taste
½ tsp *chaat masala* or to taste
juice of ½ lemon
lettuce leaves to serve

Bring a saucepan of salted water to the boil. Add the raw bean sprouts and cook until tender but al dente, about 15–20 minutes. Drain and cool. Mix with the remaining ingredients except the lettuce leaves. Taste and adjust the seasoning or spices if necessary. Allow the flavours to develop for at least 20 minutes, if possible. Serve on a bed of lettuce.

easy vegetable patties
SABZI KI TIKKI

These nutritious vegetable patties are crisp on the outside with a soft, creamy interior. If they are not hot enough for you, add green chillies and garam masala. Serve them as burgers with ketchup and some low-fat cream cheese or the more authentic *Green Chutney* (p. 184). Alternatively, make a quick sauce by cooking up 1 tablespoon of *Everyday Curry Paste* (p. 28) with some water and a little garlic, and season to taste. These can be made in advance but bring back to room temperature before cooking. Alternatively, freeze, layered with greaseproof paper.

Makes 3–4 patties (quantities can be doubled)

2 medium carrots, peeled and coarsely grated

150g (5 oz) frozen cut green or French beans, roughly sliced

1 slice of brown bread

100g (3½ oz) new potatoes, boiled or microwaved until tender and peeled

½ tsp fresh ginger, minced

½ tsp each garam masala and dried mango powder

1 good pinch of red chilli powder or to taste

3 tbs chopped fresh coriander

1 tsp salt or to taste

1 tbs vegetable oil

Cook, steam (or microwave) the carrots and beans, covered, until very soft or almost mushy (about 20 minutes on the hob in a little salted water). Stir occasionally and make sure there is enough water in the pan to stop them burning. Once cooked, uncover and dry off any excess moisture over a high heat.

Crumb the bread, either by hand or in a food processor. Pulse the potatoes with the crumbs and all the remaining ingredients except the oil in the food processor or mash together by hand. Taste and adjust the salt. Divide into equal portions and shape into 2.5cm (1 inch) thick patties. Chill for 10 minutes.

Heat the oil in a large non-stick frying pan. Add the patties, and reduce the heat a little. Brown for 1–2 minutes, undisturbed, then carefully turn and cook the other side in the same way. Continue cooking the patties for about 1 minute per side, turning often, until they are crisp and hot all the way through. Serve hot or at room temperature.

potato, chickpea and *papri* salad
PAPRI CHAAT

Chaat is a cool, spicy dish made with practically any vegetable or fruit. This dish typifies North Indian fast food and is made in minutes at roadside stalls all around New Delhi. It has masses of flavours and textures and is the perfect cooling summer dish. *Papri*, deep-fried crisps, form its basis, but if you want to leave them out, add crunch with a few crackers broken into large pieces.

Serves 1
(quantities
can be
doubled)

6–8 *papri* (p. 46)
1 small potato, cooked, peeled, cubed and chilled
half a 200g (7 oz) can of chickpeas, drained and rinsed
3 tbs low-fat yoghurt, thinned with 1 tbs water and seasoned

½ tsp roasted cumin powder
1 small pinch of red chilli powder
salt to taste
1–2 tbs *Tamarind Chutney* (p. 188), thinned with a little water
1 tbs *Green Chutney* (p. 184)
a handful of chopped fresh coriander

Make a base with the *papri* and scatter over the potato and chickpeas. Top with the seasoned yoghurt. Sprinkle with the spices and drizzle over the chutneys. Top with the coriander and eat immediately before the yoghurt makes the *papri* soggy.

These crispy little discs form the basis of many of India's most popular street foods. They are deep-fried, which is really rare in my book, but the ingredients they are normally paired with are so healthy that *papri* are allowed and even encouraged. You can buy them in Indian shops but fresh, home-made ones always taste better and they are quick and easy to make.

crispy pastry discs
PAPRI

Makes 50 pieces

100g (3½ oz) plain flour, plus extra for rolling
½ tsp salt

1 tbs vegetable oil
6 tbs water
vegetable oil for deep frying

Put the flour and salt into a large bowl and rub in the oil until well combined. Add most of the water and mix with your hands until the mixture comes together. Knead firmly for 5 minutes until you have a stiff dough. If too stiff add more water, or more flour if too loose. Allow to rest for 15 minutes.

Taking walnut-size pieces of the dough, roll out to a thickness of about 1–2mm (less than ⅛ inch) on a lightly floured work surface. You should just be able to see your fingers through the dough when you hold it up to the light. Although you should not need any excess flour while rolling, add a little if you find the dough sticking.

Prick the sheet of dough all over with a fork. Using a 5cm (2 inch) round cutter, stamp out as many rounds as possible from the sheet but do not try to pick them up yet. First lift away the dough from around the discs and combine with the remaining dough. Finally, lift up the discs and set aside. Repeat until you use up all the dough, re-rolling the scraps.

Heat the oil in a large pan or wok to a moderate temperature. The oil is hot enough when a piece of dough sizzles without browning too quickly or sinking to the bottom of the pan. Deep-fry the discs, about 2–3 minutes per batch, being careful not to overcrowd the pan and turning them over a few times. When they reach a golden caramel colour, lift out and drain on kitchen paper. Leave to cool before using. Store in an airtight container for up to 1 week.

semolina pilaff
UPPMA

This southern speciality is traditionally eaten for breakfast although I mainly eat it as a light lunch. Peanuts are often included for extra texture. You can also add cooked, diced vegetables for a more substantial meal. Serve on its own or with *Vegetable and Lentil Curry* (p. 144).

Makes 1 small portion (quantities can be doubled)

1 tsp vegetable oil
½ tsp brown mustard seeds
1 tsp peanuts
1 tsp Bengal gram (*channa dal*)
5–6 fresh or dried curry leaves
100ml (3½ fl oz) hot water

salt to taste
1–2 small, dried red chillies, crumbled
40g (1½ oz) semolina (preferably coarse-grain)
1 tsp lemon juice or to taste

Heat the oil in a small non-stick pan. Turn the heat down and add the mustard seeds, peanuts and lentils. Stir for 15 seconds and add the curry leaves. Stir for another 20 seconds and add the water, salt and chilli. Bring to the boil.

Sprinkle in the semolina and stir constantly to stop any lumps forming. Lower the heat and leave undisturbed until all the water has dried off, about 3 minutes.

Stir in the lemon juice, fluff up with a fork and serve hot.

pea-filled potato cakes
ALOO TIKKI

As you walk through the bustling markets of New Delhi, you can't ignore the inviting aromas emanating from vendors' stalls of these fresh potato cakes and their spicy filling. They are typical street fare, quick and easy to make and quite irresistible. Serve piping hot with *Green* and *Tamarind Chutneys* (pp. 184 and 188) or tomato ketchup.

Makes 3 cakes (quantities can be doubled)

250g (9 oz) waxy new potatoes, boiled in salted water until tender and peeled
1 tsp cornflour
1 tbs + ½ tsp vegetable oil
40g (1½ oz) shelled green peas, fresh or frozen, cooked until tender and drained

2 good pinches each of coriander, red chilli and cumin powders
½ tsp dried mango powder
salt to taste
1 tbs chopped fresh coriander

Dry the potatoes and grate coarsely. Add the cornflour and mix just to combine. It will be a little sticky. Refrigerate until firm enough to handle, about 15 minutes.

Heat the ½ teaspoon of oil in a small frying pan and add the peas and all the herbs and spices. Toss for about 1 minute in the pan and take off the heat. Mash a little.

Divide the potato mixture into 6 equal portions. Slick your palms with a little oil and roll each portion into a ball. Flatten into a disc 1cm (½ inch) thick. Repeat with the remaining portions. Divide the stuffing in 3 and place one portion in the middle of 3 of the cakes. Sandwich with the other 3 cakes and press the edges together to enclose the filling. Flatten and shape again.

Heat the tablespoon of oil until hot in a small non-stick frying pan. Add the cakes and cook on one side for 1–2 minutes, then turn and brown the other side. Lower the heat and cook, turning often, until well browned and crisp. Serve hot with your choice of chutney.

Once you try this recipe, eggs any other way will seem bland. I prefer not to add many spices as they overpower the delicate flavour of the eggs. If you are a diehard spice fan, add a pinch of garam masala. Serve with toast, *roti* (p. 34), rice or even *Pea-Filled Potato Cakes* (p. 48) for a wheat-free meal. The dish originated in the days when there were no toasters in India, so the bread was warmed in the same pan in which the eggs were cooked. The bread does not become crisp but heats through, soaking up the flavours left in the pan. The omelette is then sandwiched between the warmed bread slices and eaten. I still make it the same way. A must-try!

indian omelette
OMLET

Serves 1
(quantities
can be
doubled)

1 tsp vegetable oil
½ small onion, finely chopped
½ small tomato, finely chopped
½ green chilli, seeded and sliced or
   1 pinch of red chilli powder
(optional)

2 eggs, beaten with 1 pinch of salt
salt to taste
1 tbs chopped fresh coriander

Heat the oil in a small non-stick frying pan. Combine all the remaining ingredients, beat lightly and pour into the hot oil. Cook over a moderate heat, stirring, for the first 30 seconds or so until the omelette starts to set.

Once the underside has browned (30–40 seconds), carefully turn over and cook for 1 further minute or so. The centre may be slightly soft but not melting as it is with Western versions.

Fold in half and serve hot with toast and ketchup.

creamy lentil 'risotto'

KHICHERI

Khicheri is a rice and lentil dish often made in its simplest form for the weak as it is easy to digest and very nutritious. It can be soupy or thick enough to stand your spoon up in. The unusual use here of brown rice gives the dish a nutty flavour, while evoking memories of Western-style butter-laden risotto. You can keep it simple and leave out the onion, ginger, chilli and garam masala, or you can add some extra vegetables for texture and a knob of butter at the end for added creaminess. Eat with a big bowl of plain yoghurt and your favourite pickle. If you are preparing this dish in advance, remember that it thickens as it cools, so you may need to add a little more water when you reheat it.

If you prefer white rice, use (yellow) split and skinned mung beans (*dhuli hui moong dal*). Soak the rice and lentils for 30 minutes. Follow the recipe below, except that you should use only enough water to cover them by 2.5cm (1 inch) and cook on the lowest heat possible for no more than 20–30 minutes or until the rice and lentils are no longer completely distinct.

Serves 1 (quantities can be doubled)

30g (1 oz) brown rice, washed in several changes of water
30g (1 oz) lentils or split mung beans (*moong dal*)
1 tsp vegetable oil
½ tsp cumin seeds
½ small onion, sliced
1 green chilli, left whole

5–6 shreds of peeled fresh ginger
500ml (18 fl oz) hot water
salt and freshly ground black pepper to taste
2 good pinches each of turmeric powder and garam masala
1 tsp lemon juice or to taste

Soak the rice and lentils or mung beans for at least 30 minutes and up to 2 hours. Drain.

Heat the oil in a medium to large non-stick saucepan. Add the cumin and onion, and sauté over a moderate heat until just coloured, about 3–4 minutes. Add the chilli and ginger, stir and follow with the rice, lentils or mung beans, water, salt and pepper and spices. Bring to the boil for 2–3 minutes, then turn the heat down as low as possible, cover and simmer until the rice and lentils are tender, around 35 minutes (depending on the brand of rice).

Once they are tender, remove the lid and cook until the rice has a thick porridge-like consistency, mashing some of the rice and lentils with the back of a spoon. If wished, mash the cooked chilli too, which will have tamed with the cooking. Stir often, adding a splash of hot water for a thinner consistency or increase the heat to thicken, as necessary. Stir in the lemon juice, adjust the seasoning, and serve hot.

This dish is one of my favourites. It is so easy and quick to make and not at all spicy, perfect for the uninitiated. I prefer chicken breast for speed but use any joint you like, as long as it is skinned.

quick yoghurt and herb chicken
JHATTPATTA HARA MURGH

Serves 1
(quantities
can be
doubled)

1½ tsp vegetable oil
½ small onion, chopped
½ scant tsp each ginger and
   garlic pastes
1 good pinch each of turmeric and
   red chilli powders
½ tsp coriander powder

salt to taste
1 small chicken breast, skinned,
   trimmed and cubed
2 generous tbs low-fat yoghurt, beaten
½ tsp garam masala
1 heaped tbs each chopped fresh mint
   and coriander

Heat the oil in a small non-stick pan, add the onion and gently sauté until brown, about 6–7 minutes.

Add the ginger and garlic pastes, and cook for 30 seconds. Add the turmeric, chilli, coriander powder, salt and a splash of water. Cook for 1 minute.

Increase the heat, add the chicken and brown for 2–3 minutes. Stir in the yoghurt, a tablespoonful at a time, and simmer until the chicken is tender, about 4 minutes. Add splashes of hot water if necessary. When the chicken is done, increase the heat and toss in the gravy for 2–3 minutes while reducing the amount of liquid in the pan. This stage adds colour and depth to the gravy and really does improve the dish.

Stir in the garam masala, a splash of water from the kettle and the fresh herbs. Serve hot.

This is definitely a hybrid of cultures but one that works beautifully. The mushrooms are mildly spiced to provide a background flavour, which is then lifted with the coriander and mint for a fresh finish. Also great on toast.

warm, spiced mushroom salad
KHUMBI KA SALADE

Makes enough for 2 (quantities can be doubled)

1 tsp vegetable oil
½ tsp butter
½ small onion, sliced
1 level tsp garlic paste
½ tsp fresh ginger, chopped
½ tsp turmeric powder
1 tsp coriander powder
salt to taste
1 good pinch of red chilli powder
300g (10½ oz) mushrooms (any kind), thickly sliced

1 medium tomato, roughly chopped
2 tbs low-fat yoghurt, beaten
½ tsp garam masala
½ tsp dried mango powder
1 tbs chopped fresh mint
a handful of roughly chopped fresh coriander
soft lettuce leaves to serve

Melt the oil and butter together in a medium non-stick frying pan. Add the onion and cook until just golden, about 6–8 minutes. Add the garlic paste and ginger, and cook for 30–40 seconds before stirring in the turmeric, coriander powder, salt and chilli powder.

Follow with the mushrooms and toss well to mix. Cover and cook for 2–3 minutes, adding a splash of water if necessary, until softened. Add the tomato and yoghurt and cook over a moderate heat until the tomato has softened, about 3–4 minutes.

Add the remaining spices and herbs, taste and adjust the seasoning. Serve warm on the lettuce or piled onto toast.

THESE DAYS WE have no time. No time for hobbies, for friends or for ourselves. In fact, time has become the ultimate luxury. When it comes to food, we are torn. By mealtime we are starving and want something hot and tasty waiting for us on the table. But as this only happens if you are living with your mum, many of us resort to high-fat takeaways or processed food.

Enter the humble supermarket. I'm a touchy-feely person and am forever exploring supermarket aisles in search of new products that cut down my time in the kitchen. You can pick up so many store-cupboard standbys: canned beans, pots of yoghurt, frozen and canned vegetables, chilled foods and prepared foods. On the whole, I prefer to cook with fresh ingredients but it is great to be able to produce a variety of meals without having to worry about use-by dates or last-minute trips to the market.

TAKE A **CAN/PACK** OF . . .

My parents still believe that I scrimp on my nutrition when I use canned or frozen foods. However, many vegetables are frozen just after they have been picked, so they retain much of their inherent nutrition, whereas much 'fresh' produce takes a week to get to you and, like Hansel and Gretel's breadcrumbs, loses a little goodness every step of the way.

This chapter contains recipes and ideas on how to create delicious Indian-inspired dishes in no time with frozen and canned foods. (Some of the recipes in other chapters also make use of frozen products.) It is definitely not the poor relative of the other chapters. All these dishes are based on authentic recipes and most of your guests will have no idea as to whether the food is fresh or not. Having said that, you can use fresh ingredients in these recipes instead of canned ones, but remember that canned ingredients are already cooked, so you must cook fresh ones first.

Really, these are the ultimate recipes, quick and easy to make, delicious and healthy.

Spinach is one of the best vegetables to buy frozen as you don't have to clean, pick and wash it first. It works wonderfully in this easy, simple and healthy dish that is surprisingly creamy. It is the easiest spinach dish ever. As well as with Indian food, I eat it with everything: folded in an omelette, on top of roasted mushrooms or as a pancake filling. The butter adds an extra richness to the dish. Unless you have the patience and strength to grind the spinach in a pestle and mortar, you will need a food processor or blender.

simply spiced spinach
PAALAK KA SAAG

Serves 4

600g (1 lb 5½ oz) frozen chopped
   spinach or fresh spinach, picked
   over, washed and chopped
2 medium tomatoes, roughly chopped
3 fat garlic cloves, roughly chopped
½ small onion, roughly chopped
5cm (2 inch) piece of fresh ginger,
   peeled and roughly chopped

1–2 green chillies,
   left whole or seeded
salt to taste
2 tsp gram flour (*besan*)
1 good pinch of garam masala
juice of ½ lemon or to taste
1 rounded tsp butter

Place the spinach, tomatoes, garlic, onion, ginger, chilli and salt in a saucepan. Cover and simmer for 15–20 minutes, stirring occasionally. Uncover and reduce most of the excess water over a high heat. Cool slightly, then purée in a food processor or with a hand blender. Return to the pan.

Sprinkle over the flour and stir into the pan. Cook for another 4–5 minutes, adding more water if necessary. The spinach should be thick but still a purée. Stir in the garam masala, lemon juice to taste and the butter. Serve hot.

The potatoes in this dish are normally deep-fried but using canned potatoes allows us to cook them in no time with just a small amount of oil. However, it is still rich and satisfying with robust flavours. It takes only minutes to cook and is really, really tasty. Use fresh new potatoes if you have them; parboil them first in salted water and finish cooking them in the curry. Alternatively, using canned spuds can save a lot of aggravation.

spicy kashmiri potatoes
DUM ALOO

Serves 2 as part of a full meal (quantities can be doubled)

2 tsp vegetable oil
1 green chilli, left whole
1 garlic clove, grated
2 tbs *Everyday Curry Paste* (p. 28)
½ tsp red chilli powder
salt to taste
150ml (5 fl oz) hot water
3 tbs low-fat yoghurt, beaten
300g (10½ oz) can new potatoes, drained, washed and pricked all over, or the same quantity of fresh new potatoes, parboiled

1 tsp dried fenugreek leaves, crumbled
1½ tsp fennel seeds, pounded in a pestle and mortar
½ tsp garam masala
a handful of chopped fresh coriander (leaves and stalks)

Heat the oil in a small non-stick saucepan and sauté the chilli and garlic for 30 seconds. Add the curry paste, chilli powder, salt and water. Bring to the boil and simmer over a moderate heat for 4–5 minutes.

Stir in the yoghurt, a tablespoonful at a time, and cook for 3 minutes. Add the potatoes and simmer for 5 minutes. There should be enough gravy in this dish to coat the potatoes with 1 extra tablespoon per person.

Stir in the fenugreek, fennel seeds, garam masala and coriander. Cook for 1 further minute and serve hot.

spicy chickpea salad
CHOLLE KI CHAAT

This fresh and spicy salad is full of interesting flavours and contrasting textures. The earthy and mushy chickpea works wonderfully with the bite of the fresh onion, juicy tomatoes and the piquant spices. It makes a great accompaniment to any meal. Serve at room temperature on a bed of lettuce, or rolled in a *roti* (p. 34) for a quick snack, or stuff into pitta bread with a dollop of *Cucumber and Mint Yoghurt Salad* (p. 181) for a light lunch.

Serves 2
as part of a
light meal
and 4 as part
of a full meal

200g (7 oz) can chickpeas, drained
    and rinsed
½ small onion, finely chopped
1 medium tomato, roughly diced
1 green chilli, seeded and finely
    chopped (optional)
1 level tsp *chaat masala*
1 rounded tsp roasted cumin powder

2–3 tsp lemon juice or to taste
a good handful of chopped fresh
    coriander
½ tsp freshly ground black pepper
salt to taste
lettuce leaves and lemon wedges
    to serve

Toss everything together, bearing in mind that the *chaat masala* is salty so adjust the seasoning at the end. This salad improves with 2–3 hours' rest to allow the flavours to develop.

The inherent sweetness of the peas is heightened when enveloped in these spices. This recipe is based on one of my mother's favourite party dishes. It is quick and easy to make and always has the guests asking for the recipe. North Indians do not like too much sweetness in their food so will normally use fresh peas, which seem to be less sweet. Fresh or frozen, both are full of goodness and delicious in this recipe.

spicy peas
MASALEDAR MATTAR

1½ tbs vegetable oil

5cm (2 inch) piece of fresh ginger, peeled and cut into shreds

400g (14 oz) shelled fresh green peas or frozen peas, thawed

1–2 green chillies, seeded and sliced or left whole for flavour without heat

1 rounded tbs coriander powder

salt to taste

1 tsp cumin seeds

1½ tsp dried mango powder

½ tsp garam masala

1 tbs lemon juice or to taste

a handful of chopped fresh coriander to garnish

Serves 4

Heat the oil in a non-stick frying pan and fry the ginger over a moderate heat until just coloured. Add the peas, chillies, coriander powder and salt. If using fresh peas, add 100ml (3½ fl oz) water, cover and cook until the peas are tender, about 10 minutes. Frozen peas need only 4–5 minutes with a splash of water.

Uncover and dry off all the moisture in the pan. Add the remaining spices and lemon juice. Garnish with the fresh coriander. Serve hot.

corn with coconut
BHUTTA AUR NARIEL KI SABZI

This dish is mild but is a taste sensation nonetheless. Plump kernels of sweetcorn are braised in a deceptively creamy sauce and topped with a smattering of coconut for richness, flavour and texture. Great for children and the less adventurous. It is not meant to be too salty and I like to add a touch of sugar to bring out the natural sweetness of the kernels.

2 tsp unsalted butter

1 tsp brown mustard seeds

12 fresh or dried curry leaves

1–2 small dry red chillies, left whole

1 tsp fresh ginger, chopped

350g (12 oz) frozen or canned sweetcorn, drained and rinsed

1 pinch each of salt and granulated or caster sugar (optional)

250ml (9 fl oz) milk (any kind)

1 tsp lemon juice or to taste

2 tbs unsweetened flaked or desiccated coconut

Serves 3-4

Heat the butter in a small non-stick saucepan. Gently fry the mustard seeds, curry leaves, chillies and ginger for 30–40 seconds or until the seeds stop popping.

Add the sweetcorn and a little salt and sugar, if using, and stir for 2–3 minutes. Then add the milk, bring to the boil and simmer for about 10 minutes until there is no moisture left in the pan. Stir in the lemon juice and coconut, and serve hot.

Quorn, a relatively new product in the UK, is an excellent source of protein and very low in fat. This vegetarian mince has the texture and flavour of mincemeat and once cooked is indistinguishable from the real thing. I promise you that I have had unrelenting carnivores unknowingly tucking in with gusto. Use vegetarian mince if you cannot find quorn. If you are lactose intolerant, leave out the yoghurt and add extra lemon juice. Any leftovers can be used to fill samosas (p. 106), stuff flat-bread (p. 176) or as a topping for spaghetti, mixed with a little tomato sauce.

quorn mince with peas
QUORN KEEMA

1 tbs vegetable oil

100g (3½ oz) shelled green peas, fresh
   or frozen

350g (12 oz) packet quorn or
   vegetarian mince

4 tbs *Everyday Curry Paste* (p. 28)

1 rounded tsp garlic paste

salt to taste

2 tsp tomato purée

½ tsp red chilli powder

200ml (7 fl oz) hot water

2 tbs low-fat yoghurt, beaten

½ tsp garam masala

1½ tsp cumin powder

juice of ½ lemon or to taste

a handful of chopped fresh coriander
   (leaves and stalks)

Serves 4

Heat the oil in a large non-stick saucepan. Add the peas and mince, and stir-fry over a moderate to high heat for 2–3 minutes.

Add the curry and garlic pastes, salt, tomato purée, chilli powder and water, bring to the boil, cover and simmer for 15 minutes.

Uncover and stir in the yoghurt. Although this is a 'dry' dish, there should be at least 1–2 tablespoons of liquid in the mince to keep it moist, so, if necessary, add a little extra water from the kettle.

Stir in the garam masala, cumin powder, lemon juice and coriander and cook for a further minute. Serve hot.

lotus root with gram flour
BHEH

Lotus root is a fantastic long tubular vegetable commonly eaten in parts of the Orient. The spices used here completely transform it into an entirely new taste experience that is wholly different from the more familiar Chinese dishes. This is one of my favourite dishes and the only way I like lotus root; I get really excited whenever I spot some in the market. You can now buy this vegetable ready-prepared and frozen, or cooked and canned. I do prefer the frozen ones for taste and texture but either will be fine.

450g (1 lb) prepared lotus roots, cut on the slant into pieces 5mm (¼ inch) thick
2 tbs vegetable oil
1 rounded tbs gram flour (*besan*), sifted
2 level tsp each coriander and dried mango powders
½ tsp turmeric powder
½ tsp red chilli powder
½ tsp carom seeds, pounded in a pestle and mortar
salt to taste
1 rounded tsp cumin powder
½ tsp garam masala
a handful of chopped fresh coriander (leaves and stalks)

Serves 4

If using canned lotus roots, wash in several changes of water. If using fresh or frozen, peel and boil in salted water until they are tender but still retain some bite, about 15–20 minutes. To test, you should be able to break off a little from the side of a piece without too many strings or too much effort. Drain into a colander and set aside.

Heat the oil in a large non-stick frying pan. Add the flour and stir constantly over a low to moderate heat to prevent it from burning. It will look a little powdery. If necessary use a wooden spoon to break up any lumps. It is cooked when fragrant and a couple of shades darker, about 10 minutes over a low heat.

Stir in the coriander, dried mango, turmeric and chilli powders, the carom seeds and salt. Add the lotus roots and stir-fry for 3–4 minutes, coating well in the spices.

Stir in the cumin powder, garam masala and fresh coriander. Serve hot.

JUST THE **TWO** OF US

MANY OF US live with a partner, friend, sibling, child or parent and it often seems like too much bother to cook for just two people. You end up living off a diet of takeaways and convenience food, cold cereal and sandwiches and you forget how simple cooking can be. It really doesn't have to be either painful or complicated.

The recipes in this chapter are easy to make, and apart from the basic spices (which you should keep on hand anyway) use easy-to-find ingredients, store-cupboard staples and items lying around in the fridge. The quantities are mainly for two, sometimes generously so – you have no excuse to avoid the kitchen.

Double the quantities in the recipes if there are more of you and, likewise, you can scale down the quantities of most of the dishes in the other chapters. Have a look at the recipes in the Lazy Grazer chapter to knock up very quick meals and snacks, as well as those in the Leftovers? chapter, and kill two meals with one stone.

This dish is so simple and is ideal when you both eat at different times as, once prepared, the individual parcels can be cooked separately to order. A flavourful dish, perfect for a light meal with plain boiled rice. I use firm-fleshed, white fish such as halibut, haddock or even monkfish. The chilli powder is optional, as there is already a little in the curry paste. Serve with *Spicy Kashmiri Potatoes* (p. 58) and *Spicy Peas* (p. 61) for a fish-and-chips-style meal.

oven-baked spicy fish
MASALEDAR MACHCHI

**Serves 2
(quantities
can be
doubled)**

175g (6 oz) thick-cut fish steaks,
   rinsed and dried
salt to taste
3 rounded tbs *Everyday Curry Paste*
   (p. 28)
2 pinches each of freshly ground
   black pepper, garam masala,
   fenugreek seeds (pounded in a
   pestle and mortar) and red chilli
   powder

a handful of chopped fresh coriander
   (leaves and stalks)
1 tsp vegetable oil
lemon juice to taste

Make two rectangles of doubled aluminium foil 30cm × 25cm (12 inches × 10 inches) and rub the inner surface with a little oil. Season the fish, then smear the curry paste evenly over both sides. Place in the middle of foil squares, sprinkle each with the spices and coriander. Drizzle half the oil over each steak. Seal in the foil by bringing up the edges and crimping together, so that the parcel is airtight but loose.

Marinate in the fridge for at least 30 minutes and up to 3–4 hours. Bring back to room temperature before cooking.

Preheat the oven to 180°C/350°F/Gas 4. Place the parcels on a baking tray and bake for 8 minutes. Open the parcel to allow any excess liquid to dry off and continue baking for another 4–7 minutes (depending on the type and thickness of steak) until the fish is done. Drizzle over lemon juice to taste and serve hot.

coriander and coconut fish parcels
PATRANI MACHCHI

This regional dish is full of aromatic flavours. Traditionally a firm white fish (I use halibut) is steamed in a banana leaf, but I normally wrap it in a double layer of foil and bake it in the oven.

1 lemon
150g (5 oz) firm white fish fillets, rinsed and patted dry
salt to taste
freshly ground black pepper
1 tsp vegetable oil
2 banana leaves, softened in a little water, or 2 large squares of aluminium foil

PASTE
3 fat garlic cloves, roughly chopped
½ tsp ginger paste
½ small onion, roughly chopped
4 tbs chopped fresh coriander (leaves and stalks)
2 rounded tbs coconut milk powder
1 green chilli, seeded and chopped
1 tsp coriander powder
½ tsp each roasted cumin powder and garam masala
2 pinches each of carom and fenugreek seeds, pounded in a pestle and mortar

Serves 2

Cut the lemon in half. Thinly slice one half of the lemon and put aside. Squeeze the juice from the other half. Marinate the fish in 2 teaspoons of the juice, together with a good sprinkling of salt, at room temperature for 30 minutes.

Blend, process or use a pestle and mortar to pound together the ingredients for the paste into a coarse purée. If cooking in the oven, preheat to 180°C/350°F/Gas 4.

Rinse the fillets and pat dry. Season on both sides and spread a thick coating of the paste on only one side. Lay a couple of lemon slices on to each leaf or piece of foil and place the fish on top, paste side up. Grind a little black pepper over them and drizzle with the oil. Enclose in the leaf, securing with a toothpick or string, or seal in the foil by bringing up the edges and crimping together so that the parcel is airtight but loose.

Lay the parcels in a steamer above a large pan of boiling water, cover with a tight-fitting lid and steam for 15 minutes or until cooked. Alternatively, bake in the preheated oven for 10 minutes, depending on the size of the fillets. Trickle over a little of the remaining lemon juice and serve hot.

yoghurt chicken
DAHI WALA MURGH

This dish is subtle and creamy and not at all tart. It's also great made in large quantities for a party as it is loved by all, whether diehard spice junkies or curious first-timers. Serve with *roti* (p. 34) rather than rice as the gravy is thick and luscious, and robust Indian bread works well with these savoury flavours.

Serves 2 generously (quantities can be doubled)

350g (12 oz) chicken joints, skinned, rinsed, dried and pricked all over
1 tbs vegetable oil
1 small onion, finely chopped
1 green chilli, seeded and sliced
100ml (3½ fl oz) hot water
salt to taste
½ tsp black peppercorns, pounded in a pestle and mortar
½ tsp garam masala
a handful of chopped fresh coriander (leaves and stalks)

a knob of butter (optional)
1 tsp lemon juice

MARINADE
100ml (3½ fl oz) low-fat yoghurt, beaten
1 tsp ginger paste
2 tsp garlic paste
2 tsp coriander powder
½ tsp each garam masala and salt

In a non-metallic bowl mix together the marinade ingredients. Add the chicken and leave for as long as possible, in the fridge. Bring back to room temperature.

Heat the oil in a non-stick saucepan and brown the onion, around 8–10 minutes. Add the chilli and the chicken pieces, reserving the marinade, and sear over a moderate heat for 4–5 minutes.

Stir the water into the marinade and pour into the pan with a little salt. Bring to the boil, then lower the heat, cover and simmer until the joints are tender, around 25–35 minutes. Stir occasionally, making sure there is always enough water in the pan.

When the chicken is just done, increase the heat and toss in the gravy for 6–8 minutes. This intensifies the flavours and reduces the gravy to a thick consistency. Add a splash of water from the kettle so that it does not reduce too much. Add the remaining spices, coriander and butter, if using. Taste, adjust the seasoning and add the lemon juice, if necessary.

This easy chicken dish is one I invented, mixing flavours from both North and South. It is simple to make and so delicious, more savoury than spicy. I guarantee that you'll love it. The curry paste adds a deeper flavour but it's not essential. If you wish, add a squeeze of tomato purée or go a little heavier on the spice, although this dish can stand on its own merits.

easy chicken with mustard seeds
RAI AUR PYAAZ KA MURGH

Serves 2 (quantities can be doubled)

1 tbs vegetable oil
½ small onion, sliced
½ tsp brown mustard seeds, pounded
   in a pestle and mortar
1 tsp garlic paste
½ tsp turmeric powder
½ tsp chilli powder or to taste
½ tsp coriander powder
salt to taste
300g (10½ oz) chicken joints, skinned
   and rinsed

100ml (3½ fl oz) hot water
2 generous tbs low-fat yoghurt, beaten
1 heaped tsp *Everyday Curry Paste*
   (p. 28) – optional
½ tsp garam masala
freshly ground black pepper to taste
a handful of chopped fresh coriander
   (leaves and stalks)

Heat the oil in a small non-stick pan and gently fry the onion until golden. Add the mustard seeds and garlic paste, and stir for 20 seconds. Add the turmeric, chilli, coriander powder and salt, and stir for another 20 seconds.

Add the chicken and sear all over. Add the water, bring to the boil, then turn down the heat, cover and cook until nearly done, about 15 minutes.

Stir in the yoghurt, a tablespoonful at a time, until well incorporated. Add the curry paste (if using). Increase the heat and toss the chicken in the gravy for 5 minutes, adding more water if necessary. The gravy will take on a darker colour and depth, and there should be 2–3 tablespoons of it in the final dish.

Stir in the garam masala, black pepper and fresh coriander and serve hot.

'How can you possibly make something so low in fat taste this good?' my father asked me (honestly!) after just having tasted this dish. He barely realised that it was different from the dish we had been eating since I was a child. It really is superb and seriously easy to make, despite the lengthy list of ingredients. Once dried, pomegranate seeds become tangy and tart and impart an indescribable flavour to anything they are added to.

chops with dried pomegranate
ANARDHANA WALE CHOPPE

Serves 2
(quantities
can be
doubled)

4 lamb chops, all visible fat removed
2 tsp vegetable oil
1 small onion, finely chopped
1 tsp garlic paste
salt to taste
1 tsp dried mango powder
125ml (4½ fl oz) hot water
½ tsp ground black peppercorns
a handful of chopped fresh coriander
    (leaves and stalks)

MARINADE

1 tbs dried pomegranate powder
½ tsp red chilli powder
1 tsp garam masala
1 tsp white wine vinegar
1 tsp vegetable oil
2 tsp coriander powder
2 tsp garlic paste
1 tsp ginger paste
1 green chilli, seeded and sliced
    (optional)

Combine all the ingredients for the marinade in a non-metallic bowl. Add the chops and rub the mixture into them. Marinate for as long as possible, preferably overnight, in the fridge. Bring back to room temperature.

Heat the oil in a medium non-stick saucepan. Add the onion and gently fry until golden and shrivelled, about 10 minutes. Add the garlic paste and stir for a few seconds before adding the chops (reserving the marinade), salt and dried mango powder. Increase the heat and sear the meat all over for 2–3 minutes. Pour the water into the marinade, mix well and add to the pan, stirring well. Bring to the boil, cover and simmer over a low heat until the lamb is tender, about 40 minutes. Stir occasionally, adding splashes of water from the kettle when necessary.

Once the chops are tender, increase the heat and toss them in the gravy for 6–8 minutes, adding a little hot water if necessary. The gravy should be thick. Adjust the seasoning, stir in the black peppercorns and coriander and serve hot.

lamb with pickling spices
AACHAARI GOSHT

This recipe is perfect and foolproof, needing minimal preparation and very little care as it cooks. It is also one of the tastiest recipes in the book with a spectrum of complex flavours. Why not double the quantities and cook it for friends? You can substitute lemon juice for the yoghurt if you prefer but please do try to pick up a bottle of mustard oil as it results in a better dish.

Serves 2 (quantities can be doubled)

1 tbs mustard or vegetable oil
½ tsp each cumin, brown mustard, fennel, nigella (onion) and fenugreek seeds
1 small onion, roughly sliced
1 rounded tsp garlic paste
4cm (1½ inch) piece of fresh ginger, peeled and cut into shreds
1 green chilli, halved lengthways
1 rounded tsp coriander powder
225g (8 oz) lean lamb, boned, cubed, rinsed and patted dry

salt to taste
400ml (13 fl oz) hot water
2 generous tbs low-fat yoghurt, beaten, or lemon juice
lemon juice to taste
½ tsp black peppercorns, crushed in a pestle and mortar
½ tsp garam masala
a handful of chopped fresh coriander (leaves and stalks)

Heat the oil in a large, heavy-based, non-stick saucepan and stir-fry the seeds until pungent, around 40 seconds. Add the onion, garlic paste, ginger, chilli, coriander powder and meat. Stir-fry over a high heat for 2–3 minutes, then continue over a moderate heat and continue to stir-fry for about 10 minutes.

Add salt and a splash of water, cover and reduce the heat to the minimum. Stir in half the water after about 10 minutes, then continue cooking for another hour or until the lamb is tender, stirring now and then and adding splashes of hot water if necessary.

Once the lamb is cooked, add the yoghurt and remaining water, turn up the heat and toss the meat in the gravy for a final 8–10 minutes. This deepens the flavours; there should be around 2 tablespoons of sauce in the final dish.

Stir in lemon juice to taste, the black peppercorns, garam masala and fresh coriander; cook for 1 further minute and serve hot.

This is definitely the ultimate mince dish with layer upon layer of flavour that can be served with any dish and is very versatile. Buy lean mince, as ordinary mince can be very fatty. The peas can be substituted with diced carrots or potatoes, or even left out completely, although they do complement the savoury tones of the dish. Leftovers make delicious samosas (see p. 106), stuffed flatbreads (see p. 176) or a spicy shepherd's pie with the addition of mashed potato.

minced lamb with peas
MATTAR KEEMA

Serves 2–3 (quantities can be doubled)

2 tsp vegetable oil
1 tsp chopped garlic
1–2 green chillies, seeded and finely
    sliced (optional)
1 rounded tsp coriander powder
salt to taste
250g (9 oz) lean minced lamb
a good handful of shelled green peas,
    fresh or frozen

3 tbs *Everyday Curry Paste* (p. 28)
1 heaped tbs low-fat yoghurt, beaten
1 rounded tsp cumin powder
1 tsp garam masala
½ tsp freshly ground black pepper
juice of ½ lemon or to taste
a handful of chopped fresh coriander
    (leaves and stalks)

Heat the oil in a large non-stick pan, add the garlic and chillies (if using), and fry for 1 minute. Stir in the coriander powder and salt. Follow with the lamb and fresh peas (if using), and brown for 2–3 minutes.

Add the frozen peas at this point (if using), the curry paste and a good splash of water from the kettle. Stir well and bring to the boil. Reduce the heat and simmer until the lamb is done, about 8–10 minutes. Stir occasionally, breaking up any lumps that form. Add a splash of hot water if necessary. Stir in the yoghurt, the remaining dry spices and the lemon juice.

The dish should not be dry so, if necessary, add an extra splash of water from the kettle. Taste, adjust the seasoning, stir in the fresh coriander and serve hot.

dumplings in yoghurt curry
GATTE KI KADDI

If you have never tried this mild and flavourful curry, you are in for a real treat. These dumplings, made from gram flour, are unlike any others you may have tasted: robust and earthy. I insist that everyone tries them and I am never disappointed with their reactions. The gravy thickens once the dish is cooked so you may need to add a little extra water if you are reheating it later.

1 litre (1½ pints) cold water

DUMPLINGS
125g (4 oz) gram flour (*besan*)
½ tsp each dried pomegranate powder
    and whole carom seeds
½ tsp freshly ground black pepper
1 good pinch of garam masala
½ tsp salt
1 tsp vegetable oil
1 generous tbs low-fat yoghurt

CURRY
1 tsp vegetable oil
1 heaped tsp coriander powder
½ tsp cumin seeds
½ tsp turmeric powder
2 good pinches of chilli powder
salt to taste
1 medium tomato, puréed or grated
1 generous tbs low-fat yoghurt, beaten
2 good pinches of garam masala
a handful of chopped fresh coriander

Serves 2-3
(quantities
can be
doubled)

Mix together the dumpling ingredients in a large bowl. Add a couple of tablespoons of ater to bind them into a sticky mass. Wash your hands. Rub a little oil on to your palms and roll fistfuls of the dough into logs about 6cm (2½ inches) long and 2cm (¾ inch) thick. They do not have to be identical but should be similar in width.

Bring the water to the boil and add the dumplings. Stir once and cook over a moderate heat for 10 minutes. Pick up a dumpling with your spoon and if it breaks in the middle they are done. Drain, reserving the cooking liquor. Slice the dumplings into 1cm (½ inch) pieces.

Heat the oil in a medium saucepan. Add the coriander powder and cumin, and stir until fragrant, about 30 seconds. Add the turmeric, chilli powder, salt, tomato and yoghurt, and cook over a moderate heat until completely reduced, about 3–4 minutes.

Add the dumplings and about 300ml (10 fl oz) of the reserved cooking liquor. Bring to the boil and simmer for 5 minutes. Stir in the garam masala and fresh coriander.

six veg and a couple of rolls
PAO BHAJI

This spicy vegetable mash is famous on the crowded beaches of Bombay where seaside vendors knock it up to order. Traditionally, it is served with hot buttered soft bread rolls. It is meant to be thick, buttery and smooth, so omitting the butter will leave the dish slightly unfinished (although I have added only about half of the original incarnation). You will need to buy *pao bhaji masala*, the ready-made spice blend, from an Indian store, but it is inexpensive and keeps well. If you have any leftovers, save them for another day.

Serves 3

1 tbs vegetable oil
1 tsp + 2 tbs butter
1 small onion, finely chopped
½ tsp ginger paste
1 rounded tsp garlic paste
½–1 green chilli, seeded and sliced
2 tsp *pao bhaji masala*
½ tsp turmeric powder
1 tsp coriander powder
½ tsp red chilli powder
salt to taste
2 medium tomatoes,
　chopped or grated
2 tbs tomato purée
½ red or green pepper, seeded and
　finely chopped

2 medium potatoes, cooked and
　roughly mashed
150g (5 oz) cauliflower florets, cooked
　and roughly mashed
250ml (9 fl oz) hot water
1 large handful of frozen green peas,
　defrosted
2 tsp lemon juice or to taste
½ tsp garam masala
a handful of chopped fresh coriander
　(leaves and stalks)
2–3 soft white bread rolls, baps or
　hamburger rolls, to serve

Heat the oil and 1 teaspoon of the butter in a large non-stick frying pan and fry the onion until golden, about 8–10 minutes. Add the ginger, garlic and chilli, and cook for 30 seconds. Stir in the spices and cook for another 30 seconds.

Add the seasoning, tomatoes and tomato purée, cook for 4 minutes, then stir in the pepper. Cook, stirring, for 5 minutes, adding a good splash of hot water. Add the mashed vegetables and the water, bring to the boil and simmer for 8–10 minutes, mashing the vegetables further with the back of a spoon. Add the peas and the remaining butter, and cook for 2–3 minutes. The dish should be thick but sloppy, so if necessary add enough water to slacken the mixture. Taste and adjust the seasoning. Stir in the lemon juice, garam masala and fresh coriander, and cook for 1 further minute.

Halve the rolls and lightly toast the cut sides. Spread with more butter, if you like, and spoon the vegetables over each or serve alongside them.

FEW THINGS BEAT an outdoor meal; picture a table surrounded by friends, littered with fresh food and colourful pitchers, and a constant stream of inviting aromas emanating from the ol' barbie. In India the role of the barbecue is taken by a super-hot clay oven called a *tandoor* as well as by a grill set over hot coals.

A *tandoor* reaches searing temperatures and cooks food in no time while charring the exterior for that perfect barbecue flavour. Unfortunately, as they are both expensive and large, tandoori food has always been a restaurant offering but we can mimic the flavours beautifully on a domestic barbecue.

FIRE AND **SPICE**

We barbecue practically any meat, white and red, and a few hardy vegetables. These are first marinated in a medley of spices, flavourings, herbs and often yoghurt and then grilled, roasted or barbecued to succulent perfection. We are all familiar with this cuisine with its fiery colouring and unmistakable aroma but there is a lot more to Indian barbecues than this style of cooking.

The secret of success, apart from the recipe (of course), is in the marinating process. The marinade can be as simple as plain lemon juice to tenderise the meat or it can be extremely complex. Either way, the longer you leave the meat or vegetable to infuse in the marinade, the deeper the resulting flavour; the food is practically 'sauced' from within. I prepare and marinate the ingredients the night before, leave it in the fridge and cook it the following day for lunch or dinner. Minimum work, really. As with most grilled foods, these recipes are naturally low in fat – ideal for the health-conscious.

Traditionally, we serve these dishes with lemon wedges, herb chutneys, baked flat-breads and yoghurt salads. But you can also complement them with spicy American barbecue sauces, Arabic hummus, Greek taramasalata and tzatziki, flavoured low-fat mayonnaise, sweet fruit chutneys or fiery salsas, all of which work perfectly with tandoori food.

prawns with fenugreek leaves
KASTURI JHINGA

This dish is a variation on tandoori prawns. Fenugreek leaves add an extra savouriness. If you can, use fresh fenugreek, although this herb retains its extrovert personality even when dried. Large king or tiger prawns are ideal; leaving the tails on adds drama and makes them easier to eat with your fingers (is there any other way?). You can cook them under a grill, in the oven or, best of all for a charred flavour, on the barbecue.

450g (1 lb) medium or large raw prawns, washed, shelled and de-veined

3 tbs lemon juice plus extra to serve

1 pinch of salt

MARINADE

125ml (4½ fl oz) low-fat yoghurt, beaten

1½ tbs gram flour (*besan*)

1 rounded tsp ginger paste

1 tbs garlic paste

½ tsp each carom seeds and turmeric powder

2 tsp coriander powder

½ tsp red chilli powder

3 tbs dried fenugreek leaves, crumbled, or a good handful of fresh fenugreek leaves, chopped

2 tsp vegetable oil

1½ tsp garam masala

2 tsp lemon juice

salt to taste

Serves 4-6

Put the cleaned prawns in a non-metallic bowl together with the lemon juice and salt. Leave for 20 minutes. Drain and rinse them. Return to the bowl.

Whisk together all the marinade ingredients and stir into the prawns. Marinate for 2–3 hours in the refrigerator. Bring back to room temperature, discarding the marinade.

Preheat the grill or barbecue; alternatively preheat the oven to 180°C/350°F/Gas 4. Oil the rack or a baking sheet and place in the oven to preheat. Thread the prawns on to soaked wooden or metal skewers and cook for 3–4 minutes on a grill or barbecue, or 6–8 minutes in the oven, turning halfway through cooking. Drizzle with the extra lemon juice and serve hot.

tandoori-style fish
TANDOORI MACHCHI

Traditionally firm white fish fillets would be used for this classic dish. Flaky fish may not survive being barbecued and if you use a whole fish or steaks, it becomes impossible to eat this dish in the proper barbecue manner, that is, with your fingers. I often use halibut and I love the meatiness of monkfish, but use any fish you fancy.

750g (1½ lb) firm white fish fillets, rinsed and cut into 7.5cm (3 inch) cubes
lemon juice to serve

MARINADE
2 generous tbs thick-set low-fat yoghurt, beaten
1 tsp cumin seeds, pounded in a pestle and mortar
1 tbs garlic paste
2 tsp ginger paste

½ tsp carom seeds, pounded in a pestle and mortar
½ tsp each red chilli, dried mango and turmeric powders
1 tsp paprika
1 tsp tomato ketchup
1 tbs vegetable oil
½ tsp freshly ground black pepper
1 tbs gram flour (*besan*)
1 rounded tsp garam masala
1 tsp lemon juice
salt to taste

Serves 4

Whisk together the ingredients for the marinade. Taste to make sure there is enough salt and chilli. Place in a non-metallic dish and stir in the fish. Marinate for 2–3 hours if possible, in the fridge. Discard the marinade.

Preheat the oven to 180°C/350°F/Gas 4 or preheat the grill. Thread the fish on to soaked wooden or metal skewers and place on an oiled rack or oiled baking sheet. Cook until opaque, about 6–8 minutes under the grill or 10 minutes in the oven, turning halfway through cooking.

Drizzle with the lemon juice and serve hot.

These succulent kebabs take just minutes to prepare and minutes to cook. They can be made as long sausage-like kebabs and barbecued on skewers, or shaped into burgers. I often make small bite-size patties on the hob as appetisers for guests, and they are always well received. Serve with *Green Chutney* (p. 184), a refreshing yoghurt salad, pitta or *naan* bread (p. 109). For a richer, smoother kebab, I add cashew nut paste.

chicken kebabs
MURGH KE KEBAB

Serves 4–6 as kebabs or makes 20 small bite-size patties

vegetable oil for frying or grilling
lemon juice to serve

KEBABS
500g (1 lb 2 oz) minced chicken
2 tsp vegetable oil
1 medium onion, grated and squeezed
    of extra liquid
1 tbs garlic paste
2 tsp ginger paste
2–3 green chillies, seeded and
    finely chopped

1½ tsp salt
1 tsp cumin powder
2 tsp lemon juice
1 rounded tsp dried mango powder
2 good tsp cornflour or gram flour
2 tsp garam masala
2 tbs cashew nuts, soaked for
    30 minutes in boiling water and
    pounded to a paste in a pestle
    and mortar
2 handfuls of fresh coriander,
    finely chopped

Stir together all the ingredients for the kebabs in a non-metallic bowl, cover and marinate for as long as possible, preferably overnight, in the fridge. Bring back to room temperature.

Wet your hands and take a couple of handfuls of the mixture. Press around metal or soaked wooden skewers, in sausage-like shapes, or make them freeform into small burger shapes. Brush with the oil and place on the grill. Cook, turning halfway through cooking, until done, about 5–7 minutes.

Alternatively, cook on the hob. Heat 1 tablespoon of oil in a large non-stick frying pan and fry on one side until golden. Turn over, reduce the heat and cover the pan (this keeps them soft). Cook for 5–6 minutes altogether or until they are done.

Drizzle with lemon juice and serve hot.

succulent creamy chicken tikka
MURGH MALAI TIKKA

This chicken tikka is milder and smoother than the traditional dish that is synonymous with Indian food, in both spiciness and heat. Normally these kebabs would be marinated in cream and nuts. I have retained the nuts, which contain a healthy fat, but have left out the cream; the dish is still delicious without it. You can serve it as an appetiser, snack, a sandwich filling or for a main course. It is very versatile and very tasty. It can be cooked either on a grill or barbecue, or baked in the oven.

Serves 2 as a main course or 4 as appetisers (quantities can be doubled)

2 chicken breasts, skinned, boned and cubed
vegetable oil to brush the grill or baking tray
lemon juice to taste
½ tsp garam masala
sliced raw red onions, lemon wedges and fresh coriander to garnish

MARINADE
75ml (2½ fl oz) low-fat yoghurt, beaten
2 tsp mustard or vegetable oil
scant ½ tsp each turmeric, red chilli and dried mango powders

½ tsp garam masala
1 tsp dried fenugreek leaves, crumbled
2 good pinches each of carom, fennel and green cardamom seeds and black peppercorns (ground together)
2 tsp each garlic and ginger pastes
1 tbs cashew nuts, soaked in water for 30 minutes and made into a paste in a pestle and mortar
1 rounded tbs gram flour (*besan*)
1 egg yolk
½ tsp salt or to taste

Whisk together the ingredients for the marinade and tip into a plastic bag or non-metallic bowl. Taste for salt and chilli, and adjust if necessary. Pierce the chicken all over, add to the marinade and stir to coat properly. Marinate for as long as possible, preferably overnight, in the fridge. Bring back to room temperature and discard the marinade.

Preheat the oven to 200°C/400°F/Gas 6 (if using); alternatively preheat the grill and brush the rack with oil. Thread the chicken pieces on to soaked wooden or metal skewers and grill until done, about 6–8 minutes, turning every 2–3 minutes; or bake on the top shelf of the preheated oven on an oiled baking tray and cook until done, about 6–8 minutes, turning halfway through cooking and basting with extra oil. The chicken should be slightly charred at the edges.

Using a fork, slide the chicken pieces off the skewers. Squeeze over the lemon juice, sprinkle with the garam masala and serve hot with the garnishes.

Succulent Creamy Chicken Tikka on Naan *Bread*

blond tandoori chicken
TANDOORI MURGH

This famous chicken dish is loved by all. My version is 'blond' as I don't use the food colouring that gives the chicken its characteristic red, although I do add paprika for a little colour. For restaurant-quality flavour, marinate overnight. I prefer leg or thigh joints as I find the meat more flavourful and succulent but use whichever part you like and transform any leftovers into *Buttery Chicken* (p. 173).

6 chicken thigh joints, skinned and all
    visible fat removed, rinsed and
    dried
juice of 1 lemon plus extra to drizzle
½ tsp salt
2 tsp vegetable oil for drizzling
½ tsp each dried mango powder,
    garam masala, dried fenugreek
    leaves (crushed) and fenugreek
    seeds (ground in a pestle and
    mortar)
lemon wedges and fresh coriander
    leaves to garnish

MARINADE
200ml (7 fl oz) thick-set low-fat
    yoghurt, beaten
1 tsp ginger paste
1 tbs garlic paste
1 tsp each cumin and coriander
    powders
½ onion, roughly chopped
1 tsp mustard or vegetable oil
1 tsp garam masala

Serves 3

Slash the chicken at regular intervals; you can cut right down to the bone. This ensures even cooking and lets the flavour of the marinade penetrate deep into the meat. Drizzle over the lemon juice and rub in the salt. Set aside for 30 minutes. Rinse the chicken.

Meanwhile, whizz the marinade ingredients together in a food processor. (If you don't have one, grate the onion, squeeze out the excess liquid and combine with the other ingredients.) Rub into the chicken pieces. Place in a non-metallic bowl, cover and marinate for as long as possible, preferably overnight, in the fridge. Bring back to room temperature. Discard the marinade.

Preheat the grill or barbecue and brush with vegetable oil, or preheat the oven to 200°C/400°F/Gas 6 and place an oiled ovenproof dish inside to heat up. Place the chicken straight on the barbecue or grill or into the baking dish, drizzle over the oil and cook, turning halfway through cooking, until done, about 10–15 minutes on a barbecue, 15 minutes on a grill and 20 minutes in the oven. After 10 minutes, sprinkle over the remaining ground spices. If baking in the oven, finish under the grill to simulate that barbecue effect.

Drizzle with lemon juice and serve hot, garnished with the lemon wedges and the fresh coriander.

barbecued minty lamb chops
TANDOORI CHOPPE

We have been using this unusual recipe for lamb chops since as far back as I can remember and no one knows where it originated. It is absolutely delicious and I have found nothing like it anywhere else. This definitely needs to marinate overnight in the fridge. Bring back to room temperature before grilling.

Serves 6–8
as part of a
barbecue
spread

500g (1 lb 2 oz) small lamb chops
2 tbs white wine vinegar
1 small packet of fresh mint, pounded
   in a pestle and mortar to make
    2 tbs paste
1½ tsp garam masala

2 tsp each ginger and garlic pastes
½ tsp red chilli powder
1 tbs vegetable oil
1½ tsp salt
lemon juice to taste

Combine all the ingredients except the lemon juice and marinate for at least 1 hour, but preferably overnight, in the fridge. Bring back to room temperature.

Discard the marinade. Grill on a hot barbecue for 6–7 minutes per side or until done to your preference. Drizzle over the lemon juice and serve hot.

This dish is really versatile; it can be served as bite-sized snacks, as a filling for sandwiches or as part of a main course. Start it the night before for the best results. Serve with fresh *Green Chutney* (p. 184) or dip into cool *Cucumber and Mint Yoghurt Salad* (p. 181) and serve with *naan* (p. 109). Alternatively, serve on a bed of *Carrot Pilaff* (p. 163) with a bean or lentil dish.

luscious lamb brochettes
BOTI KEBAB

450g (1 lb) lean boned lamb, cut into 2cm (¾ inch) cubes and pierced with a fork
½ tsp garam masala
juice of 1 lemon

MARINADE
150ml (5 fl oz) low-fat yoghurt, beaten
½ small onion, roughly chopped

Serves 4–6

2 tsp each garlic and ginger pastes

1 tsp vegetable oil
½ tsp red chilli powder or to taste
2 tsp each cumin powder and garam masala
2–3 pinches each of fennel seeds and freshly ground black pepper
2 tbs chopped fresh coriander
2 tsp vegetable oil
1½ tsp salt or to taste

Whizz all the marinade ingredients together in a food processor until smooth and pour into either a plastic bag or a non-metallic bowl. (If you don't have a food processor, grate the onion and squeeze out the excess liquid; chop the coriander finely then pound in a pestle and mortar; finally combine with the remaining marinade ingredients.) Add the lamb, mix well and leave to marinate for as long as possible, preferably overnight, in the fridge. Bring back to room temperature 1 hour before cooking. Discard the marinade.

Thread the cubes on to soaked wooden or metal skewers and place on a preheated barbecue or griddle pan or under a preheated grill. Cook until tender, around 5–6 minutes under the grill or 8–10 minutes on a barbecue or in a griddle pan, turning halfway through cooking. Alternatively cook for 10–15 minutes in an oven preheated to 200°C/400°F/Gas 6. If you prefer your lamb pink, cook it for less time. Sprinkle with the extra garam masala, drizzle over the lemon juice and serve hot.

Luscious Lamb Brochettes with a bowl of Cucumber and Mint Yoghurt Salad.

Fenugreek has a very distinct savoury taste, and retains its character once dried; it will keep for ever if stored in a dark place.

fenugreek leavened bread
METHI KI NAAN

250g (9 oz) plain flour
a good pinch of caster sugar
1 tsp salt
2 tsp dried fast-action yeast powder
1 tsp vegetable oil plus extra for
   brushing
3 tbs low-fat yoghurt, beaten
1 small egg, beaten

up to 100ml (3½ fl oz) cold water, to bind
1 rounded tbs dried fenugreek leaves,
   crumbled, or 2 handfuls of fresh
   fenugreek leaves, washed and
   chopped
2 garlic cloves, chopped finely
½ tsp carom seeds, pounded in a
   pestle and mortar

Makes 6

Combine the flour, sugar, salt and yeast powder in a bowl. Make a well in the centre and pour in the oil, yoghurt and egg. Mix well. Add water to bind for a soft, pliable dough. Knead for 8–10 minutes. Add the remaining ingredients and knead to distribute evenly. Place the dough in a large oiled bowl. Cover and leave to prove in a warmish place until doubled in size, about 1 hour.

Heat the barbecue, grill, *tava* or frying pan to a high setting. Alternatively, preheat the oven to 200°C/425°F/Gas 7 and preheat a baking sheet.

Divide the dough into 6 pieces. Take one and cover the rest. Flour your work surface lightly and roll out the dough into a thin round (about 3–4 mm/⅛ inch) or oval shape.

Smear the dough with a tiny bit of oil and slap on to the grill or into a pan. Cook for 1 minute undisturbed, until the surface develops little air bubbles. Turn it over and cook the underside until little brown spots appear. Lower the heat a little. Keep turning the bread until cooked and charred in a few places, 1 further minute or so.

If using an oven, place the bread on the preheated baking sheet. Cook until puffed, about 1–2 minutes, then place under a preheated grill for 1 further minute or so until slightly charred in places. Serve hot.

tandoori mushrooms
TANDOORI KHUMBI

Mushrooms are often referred to as a vegetarian meat as they have a chewy texture and a comparable depth of flavour. Any barbecue spread must include mushrooms to cater for the growing number of vegetable-lovers in our midst. These stuffed mushrooms are actually really easy to make and the barbecue adds an unbeatable smoky note to the average fungi. The paste may seem strong but it needs to be to do the job.

350g (12 oz) large closed-cap mushrooms
100g (3½ oz) frozen chopped spinach, thawed
salt to taste
2 tsp vegetable oil
1 lemon, cut into wedges, to serve

PASTE
250ml (9 fl oz) low-fat yoghurt, beaten
1 tsp vegetable oil
2 tbs gram flour (*besan*)
2 tsp garlic paste
1 tsp ginger paste
½ tsp red chilli powder
1 rounded tbs garam masala
½ tsp each carom and green cardamom seeds, pounded in a pestle and mortar
1 rounded tsp cumin powder
1 rounded tsp dried fenugreek leaves, crumbled
a handful of chopped fresh coriander
salt to taste

Serves 4

Cook the mushrooms in boiling salted water until just tender, around 12–15 minutes. Drain and, when cool, remove the stems and discard.

Heat the spinach through, either in a small saucepan or in the microwave (about 2 minutes, covered). It should be dry, so boil off any extra water and squeeze out any excess. Add salt to taste and set aside.

Whisk together the ingredients for the paste. Taste to make sure there is enough salt and chilli. Preheat the barbecue or grill and brush with the vegetable oil, or place a well-oiled baking tray in an oven preheated to 230°C/450°F/Gas 8.

Tightly pack the mushroom cavities with the spinach. Dip them one by one into the paste and coat thickly. Place, filling side down, on the barbecue or the grill or baking sheet and cook, 3–4 minutes under the grill or on the barbecue or 6 minutes in the oven, turning over once the undersides are golden. Serve hot with lemon wedges.

INDIANS LOVE TO entertain. We need an excuse *not* to have a party and, whether it's intimate or large, we cook enough to feed an army. A typical spread would include one or two red or white meat dishes; one pulse and at least one vegetable dish; rice, bread or both; and the usual accompaniments of yoghurt, chutneys and pickles.

Some people like to keep their entertaining simple and easy, preferring to spend their time with friends sharing a couple of one-pot dishes; others need to impress their guests and set about creating a night and a menu that will be remembered and relished. Whichever category you fall into, there are recipes here that will suit you. I always want to treat my guests to new and exotic flavours, but invariably end up resorting to quick, easy and foolproof dishes. A few of these recipes are elaborate but most of them are very straightforward and no-fuss. All are designed to impress.

FRIENDS TO DINNER

Either way, the secret of a stress-free party is menu planning. There are two parts to this: pairing together the right dishes; and choosing those that are easy to make or can be prepared in advance. In this respect, Indian food is ideal party fare as nearly all curries, pulse dishes and desserts actually benefit from being made the day before. Bread can be made earlier in the day and reheated (see p. 15). Salad can be prepared and then simply dressed before serving. Chutneys and pickles can be bought or made earlier in the week. Another time-saving tip is to make and keep a large jar of *Everyday Curry Paste* (p. 28) in the fridge and use it to make all the curry-based dishes.

Choose recipes from any chapter. There are no rules about what you have to serve but follow the above guidelines for a traditional format. You need not worry that you are short-changing your guests by serving them these 'healthy' dishes as they are really delicious. But if you feel guilty, just add a little extra butter or oil to the recipe. Do, however, make a couple of the recipes just as they are; trust me, your guests will not suffer and you will sleep soundly.

I made this delectable, spicy curry for a kitchen full of chefs when I was working in LA. The prawns were so fresh they practically jumped into the sink but frozen prawns are just as great as long as they are raw. Medium-sized prawns are ideal but smaller ones also work well. Whatever their size, they must be raw. I use nearly all the specified amount of tamarind but adjust to suit your own taste. Serve with plain boiled rice and *Potatoes with Onions and Mustard Seeds* (p. 131).

goan prawn curry
GOA KA JHINGA CURRY

Serves 4 (quantities can be doubled)

1½ tbs vegetable oil
1 medium onion, finely chopped
1 heaped tsp garlic paste
15 fresh or dried curry leaves
3–5 dried red chillies, broken,
   or ½ tsp dried red chilli flakes or
   to taste (optional)
1 heaped tsp brown mustard seeds
5 tbs *Everyday Curry Paste* (p. 28)
500ml (18 fl oz) hot water

4 tbs coconut milk powder
450g (1 lb) raw prawns, shelled,
   washed and de-veined
1–2 tsp tamarind paste or 20–30g
   (1 oz) block of tamarind, soaked
   and juice extracted (see p. 27)
1 tsp garam masala
½ tsp each freshly ground black
   pepper and dried mango powder
salt to taste

Heat the oil in a large non-stick saucepan and brown the onion, about 10–12 minutes. Stir in the garlic paste, curry leaves, chillies (if using) and mustard seeds, and fry for 30 seconds. Add the curry paste and 100ml (3½ fl oz) of the water. Simmer for 10 minutes, adding splashes of water if necessary. Reduce before continuing.

Stir in the remaining water; bring to the boil for 3–4 minutes. Stir in the coconut powder and mix well; the lumps will disappear. Add the prawns, lower the heat, cover and simmer until the prawns are nearly cooked, about 3 minutes. The gravy should be smooth and thick, and there should be enough to eat with rice. If it is a little watery, reduce the liquid over a high heat until it has the right consistency. Add the tamarind to taste. Stir in the remaining spices, adjust the seasoning and serve hot.

pickled pink prawns
AACHAARI JHINGA

After making this dish for some guests, it was suggested that I market it to make my fortune. Needless to say, I took this as a huge compliment but never did anything about it. If anyone agrees and has the right connections, let me know . . . Meanwhile, make these spicy prawns for your friends and family and lap up the compliments yourself. Mustard oil really does add an extra element that elevates this dish to its indescribable glory and is easy to find in Indian stores.

Serves 6–7 (quantities can be halved)

3 tbs mustard or vegetable oil
2 small onions, chopped
1½ tbs each garlic and ginger pastes
2–3 green chillies, left whole, or halved lengthways and seeded
1½ tsp each brown mustard, nigella (onion), fennel, cumin and fenugreek seeds
½ tsp turmeric powder
1½ rounded tbs coriander powder
salt to taste

4 medium tomatoes, puréed
800g (1 lb 9 oz) medium to large raw prawns, washed, shelled, with the tails intact, and de-veined
100ml (3½ fl oz) hot water
2 tsp garam masala
½ tsp freshly ground black pepper
1 tbs lemon juice or to taste
a handful of chopped fresh coriander (leaves and stalks)

Heat the oil in a non-stick saucepan and gently fry the onions until golden and shrivelled, about 10 minutes. Add the garlic and ginger pastes and the chillies, and cook for 40 seconds before adding the seeds, turmeric, coriander powder and salt. Stir.

Add the tomatoes and simmer for 10 minutes, adding splashes of hot water whenever necessary. Reduce before continuing.

Add the prawns and the water. Bring to the boil, then lower the heat, cover and simmer until the prawns are nearly cooked, about 3–5 minutes. Uncover and stir over a high heat while reducing the sauce to the consistency of thick gravy. Add a splash of hot water from the kettle if necessary. There should be enough gravy to mop up with your *roti*.

Stir in the remaining spices, lemon juice and fresh coriander. Serve hot.

Pickled Pink Prawns with Roti

This dish sounds a lot hotter than it is; the overriding flavour is that of fresh black pepper rather than raw heat. But if you like it hot, the addition of green chillies works really well. On the other hand, if you wish, you can substitute some of the black peppercorns with the milder green variety for a subtler flavour.

black pepper chicken
KAALI MIRCHI WALA MURGH

1 kg (2 lb 4 oz) chicken joints, skinned and trimmed, with all visible fat removed
2 tbs vegetable oil
1 small onion, finely chopped
5cm (2 inch) piece of fresh ginger, peeled and cut into thin shreds
1 tsp garlic paste
1–2 green chillies (optional), whole for flavour, sliced to add heat
1 tbs coriander powder
salt to taste
juice of 1 lemon or to taste

½ tsp garam masala
a handful of chopped fresh coriander (leaves and stalks)

MARINADE
3 tbs garlic paste
1 tbs ginger paste
2½–3 heaped tbs black peppercorns, coarsely ground
1 tsp garam masala
1 tsp vegetable oil
1 chicken stock cube, dissolved in 3 tbs hot water

Serves 6-8

Combine the marinade ingredients and place in a non-metallic bowl. Add the chicken, mix well and marinate for at least 1 hour, or preferably overnight, in the fridge. Bring back to room temperature.

Heat the oil in a non-stick saucepan. Add the onion; sauté over a moderate heat, until quite brown, about 8 minutes. Add the ginger, garlic paste, chillies (if using), coriander powder and salt, and sauté for 30–40 seconds. Increase the heat, add the chicken (reserving the marinade) and sear all over, about 3–4 minutes.

Stir a splash of hot water into the marinade and pour into the pan. Lower the heat, cover and cook until the chicken is done, around 20–30 minutes. Stir occasionally, adding splashes of hot water whenever necessary.

Once the chicken is tender, uncover, increase the heat and toss in the gravy for a good 4–5 minutes. This will deepen the flavours. Add a splash of water to the pan if it is too dry. The final dish should have 2–3 tablespoons of gravy in it. Add the lemon juice, garam masala and fresh coriander, cook for 1 further minute and serve hot.

kashmir lamb with fennel seeds
KASHMIRI GOSHT

This delectable lamb dish is based on the cooking of Kashmir and would traditionally be made with cream or nut pastes, or both. I limit the quantity of nuts and use skimmed milk and yoghurt instead of the cream. Far from feeling deprived, you'll be licking your fingers . . .

Serves 4–6, accompanied with other dishes

2 tbs vegetable oil
1 medium onion, finely chopped
800g (1 lb 9 oz) lean stewing lamb on the bone, cubed
1 heaped tbs garlic paste
1 level tbs ginger paste
1 tbs coriander powder
½–1 tsp red chilli powder (optional)
salt to taste

125ml (4½ fl oz) each skimmed milk and low-fat yoghurt, beaten
3 tbs ground almonds
1½ tsp garam masala
1 heaped tbs fennel seeds, pounded in a pestle and mortar
a handful of chopped fresh coriander (leaves and stalks)
lemon juice to taste

Heat the oil in a non-stick saucepan and gently brown the onion, about 15 minutes.

Increase the heat, add the lamb and toss over a high heat for 4–5 minutes. Reduce the heat, add the garlic and ginger pastes, coriander powder, chilli (if using) and salt, and stir for 1 minute. Add a splash of water from the kettle, cover and simmer over a low heat until the lamb is tender, about 60–70 minutes. Stir occasionally, adding splashes of hot water when necessary.

Uncover, increase the heat and stir in the milk, yoghurt and almonds. Toss the lamb in the gravy for 10 minutes to add colour and depth and to reduce the sauce until very thick. Add more water if necessary, but do not skip this stage as the gravy really benefits. The resulting sauce should have the consistency of thick cream.

Add the remaining spices, fresh coriander and lemon juice to taste. Serve hot.

silky lamb mince patties

SHAMMI KEBAB

These patties are so smooth, light and crumbly that they just melt in the mouth. Serve with *Green Chutney* (p. 184) or *Tangy Tomato Chutney* (p. 186). You will need a food processor for this dish.

Makes 16 small patties or 8 medium-sized

1 thick slice of white bread, crumbed and toasted in a dry pan
1 rounded tsp cumin powder
1 large egg white
1–2 tbs vegetable oil

PATTIES
450g (1 lb) lean lamb mince
4 tbs Bengal gram (*channa dal*), soaked for 2–3 hours
9 cloves
½ tsp black peppercorns
2.5cm (1 inch) cinnamon stick
2 blades of mace
4 bay leaves
4 brown cardamom pods, lightly crushed
1 medium onion, roughly chopped
4cm (1½ inch) piece of fresh ginger, peeled and roughly chopped
4 large garlic cloves, roughly chopped
3 green chillies, halved lengthways and seeded
1½ tsp salt or to taste
125ml (4½ fl oz) cold water

Heat a large saucepan and add all the ingredients for the patties. Stir on a high heat for 2–3 minutes, then continue over a moderate heat, covered, until the mince is done, about 40 minutes. Then turn up the heat and dry off every last drop of moisture in the pan until meat is completely dry and crumbly; around 15 minutes. Stir constantly to prevent the lamb from catching and burning. Leave to cool slightly.

Add the breadcrumbs, cumin and egg white. Blend to a fine paste in a food processor. Turn out into a bowl, cool and chill for 2 hours or overnight.

If wished, make a little meatball, fry and taste for spices and seasoning. Adjust if necessary. (If left in the refrigerator overnight the mince will be too stiff to work with straight away and will need to soften a little at room temperature.) Knead the mince as you would dough for at least 5 minutes; the longer you work the mixture, the softer the patty. For medium-sized kebabs, take small handfuls of the mince, roll into a ball and flatten to make a 7.5cm (3 inch) burger.

Heat half the oil in a large non-stick frying pan and carefully add only enough patties to sit in one layer. Lower the heat to moderate and cook on one side without disturbing for about 4 minutes, then using a spatula turn over and cook the underside in the same way. They should be nice and crisp. Repeat with the remaining mince and oil.

Silky Lamb Mince Patties topped with Green Chutney and Tangy Tomato Chutney

yoghurt-braised lamb
DAHI GOSHT

A delicately spiced lamb dish that is deceptively easy to make. It's one of those recipes that make your friends think you are a culinary genius while you're really catching up on your reading with your feet up on the table. This dish has no chillies or garam masala, which may seem odd and bland to many palates, but give it a try.

700g (1 lb 8 oz) lean stewing or casserole lamb, cubed
300ml (10 fl oz) low-fat yoghurt, beaten
1 rounded tbs garlic paste
2 scant tsp ginger paste
1 tbs vegetable oil
1 chicken stock cube

salt to taste
1 small onion, sliced
1 small tomato, diced
100ml (3½ fl oz) hot water
1 tsp freshly ground black pepper
a handful of fresh chopped coriander (leaves and stalks)

Serves 4–5

Mix together the lamb, yoghurt and garlic and ginger pastes. Place in a non-metallic bowl and marinate for as long as possible, preferably overnight, in the fridge. Bring back to room temperature.

Heat the oil in a medium-sized saucepan. Spoon in the lamb (reserving the marinade) and brown all over, about 4–5 minutes. If the pan seems too watery, pour the liquid back into the marinade bowl and continue; eventually the meat will brown. Scrape the marinade into the pan. Crumble in the stock cube, add a little salt and stir to dissolve. Cover and cook on a very low heat, stirring occasionally, for 30 minutes. Add a splash of water whenever necessary.

Next, add the onion, cover again and cook for a further 10 minutes. Add the tomato, cover again and continue cooking until the lamb is tender and cooked through, around 20 minutes or more.

Once the lamb is cooked, add the water to the pan and then reduce by three-quarters over a high heat while tossing the meat in the gravy, about 8 minutes. This intensifies the flavours of the dish. Stir in the black pepper and coriander.

Imagine tender nuggets of lamb cooked with earthy lentils. You can substitute any meat or vegetable for the lamb.

lamb and lentil stew
GOSHT DHANSAK

Serves 6–8 with other dishes (quantities can be halved)

1 kg (2 lb 4 oz) lean stewing or casserole lamb, cubed
1–2 green chillies, whole (optional)
3 tbs vegetable oil
1 medium onion, finely chopped
1 tsp each fenugreek and black mustard seeds, pounded in a pestle and mortar
1 tbs coriander powder
½ tsp each turmeric and red chilli powders
salt to taste
50g (1¾ oz) each split pigeon peas (*toovar dal*), split mung beans (*moong dal*) and red lentils (*masoor dal*), picked over and washed
1 litre (1½ pints) hot water

½–1 tsp tamarind paste *or* 30–35g (1–1½ oz) block of tamarind, soaked and juice extracted (see p. 27) or to taste
½ tsp freshly ground black pepper
1 rounded tsp each of garam masala and cumin powder
1 rounded tsp fennel seeds, pounded in a pestle and mortar
a handful of chopped fresh coriander (leaves and stalks)

MARINADE
2 tbs garlic paste
1 tbs ginger paste
½ tsp salt
½ tsp garam masala
juice of ½ lemon

Combine the lamb with the marinade ingredients and the green chilli (if using) in a non-metallic bowl. Cover and marinate for as long as possible, preferably overnight, in the fridge. Bring back to room temperature.

Heat the oil in a large non-stick saucepan, add the onion and sauté until golden, about 10 minutes. Add the seeds, coriander, turmeric and chilli powders and salt. Add the lamb and stir-fry over a medium heat for 4–5 minutes. Scrape in the marinade.

Add the pulses and the water, bring to the boil, then simmer, covered, on the lowest heat possible until the meat is tender, around 1–1½ hours. Stir occasionally, as the pulses have a tendency to fall to the bottom of the pan. Add more hot water if necessary.

Once the lamb is tender, turn up the heat and stir for about 5 minutes to thicken the gravy. Stir in the tamarind to taste, black pepper, remaining spices and fresh coriander.

mughlai lamb and rice dish
GOSHT KI BIRYANI

This all-in-one rice and meat dish was originally brought to India by the food-and-feast-loving Moguls. Even today, biryanis are mainly served at dinner parties as a treat rather than as daily family fare. Thankfully, most of the preparation can be done the day before and the final oven-cooking completed on the day, adding an extra 5–15 minutes' cooking time. The whole spices add great flavour but you can substitute an extra half-teaspoon of garam masala. A biryani is normally garnished with fried sliced onions, fried almonds and plumped sultanas or golden raisins. Include them if you have time and want some extra glamour.

600g (1 lb 5½ oz) boned lamb or 800g (1 lb 9 oz) if on the bone, cubed
3 tbs vegetable oil
2 medium onions, chopped
2 tsp coriander powder
1½ tsp garam masala
½–1 tsp red chilli powder
½ tsp turmeric powder
salt to taste
3 tbs almonds, blanched, dried and ground, or shop-bought ground almonds
250ml (9 fl oz) hot water
275g (10 oz) long-grained white rice, washed and soaked for 30 minutes
1 tbs unsalted butter, plus a little extra
½ tsp saffron strands, soaked in 4 tbs warm milk

½ tsp *kewra* essence (optional)
juice of ½ large lemon or to taste

MARINADE
1½ tbs each ginger and garlic pastes
½ tsp freshly ground black pepper
175g (6 oz) low-fat yoghurt, beaten

WHOLE SPICES
6 cloves
3 large bay leaves
2 whole cinnamon sticks
3 brown cardamom pods, lightly crushed
5 green cardamom pods, lightly crushed
2 blades of mace (optional)

Serves 6–8 (quantities can be halved)

Pierce the lamb several times with a fork. Combine the marinade ingredients in a non-metallic bowl. Add the lamb, mix well and marinate for as long as possible, preferably overnight, in the fridge. Bring back to room temperature.

continued overleaf

Heat the oil in a large non-stick saucepan. Add the whole spices and fry until pungent, 30–40 seconds. Add the onions and brown well, lowering the heat once they start to colour, about 15 minutes.

Increase the heat, add the lamb (reserving the marinade) and brown all over, stirring often, for about 4–5 minutes. Stir in the spices and salt. Add the marinade, the ground almonds and the water. Bring to the boil, then cover and cook over the lowest possible heat until the meat is tender, about 60–70 minutes. Stir occasionally and add water from the kettle whenever necessary. When the meat is done, increase the heat and toss it in the gravy for 5–6 minutes to add extra depth and reduce any excess liquid. If necessary add extra water, but do not omit this step. The finished gravy should be thick but not coating. Set aside. (If cooking the following day, cool, cover, and refrigerate. Bring back to room temperature.)

Preheat the oven to 180°C/350°F/Gas 4. Parboil the rice in plenty of salted, boiling water until just underdone, around 4–5 minutes (if soaked). To check, crush a grain between your fingers. There should be a thin white line in the middle and the grain will still have a little bite to it. Drain and refresh in cold water to stop the cooking process.

Lightly butter a medium-sized, ovenproof casserole dish with a tight-fitting lid. Spread a thin layer of gravy over the base and cover evenly with half the rice. Drizzle with half the saffron. Top evenly with the lamb and cover with the remaining rice. Drizzle over the saffron and *kewra* essence (if using) and dot the surface with small pieces of butter. Cover the dish with foil and the lid. Bake in the preheated oven for 30 minutes or until the rice is done. The biryani will stay warm in the casserole dish for at least 20 minutes.

Squeeze over the lemon juice, and scatter over the onions, nuts and sultanas (if using). Serve hot.

buttery lentil curry
MAKHNI DAL

This dish is traditionally made with vast amounts of butter and cream and is one of northern India's favourite restaurant dishes. When I told friends that this dish featured on my healthy menu, they thought I had lost the plot. My version is creamy and meltingly smooth. No one believes it's home-made, never mind low fat.

5cm (2 inch) piece of fresh ginger, peeled

150g (5 oz) whole black gram (*ma dal*), picked over and washed several times

1–2 green chillies, left whole

1 heaped tsp garlic, chopped

½ small onion, chopped

1.2 litres (2 pints) cold water

75g (2¾ oz) canned red kidney beans

3 tbs low-fat yoghurt, beaten

1 heaped tbs tomato purée

salt to taste

1 tsp garam masala

a pinch of dried mango powder

a handful of chopped fresh coriander

TARKA

2 tsp each of unsalted butter and vegetable oil

½ small onion, chopped

1 tsp garlic paste

2 medium tomatoes, skinned and chopped

Serves 5-6

Cut half the ginger into fine shreds and finely chop the remainder. Place the lentils, chillies, garlic, onion, water and the chopped ginger in a large heavy-based saucepan. Bring to the boil, cover and cook over a very low heat until the lentils are tender, about 1 hour. Stir occasionally, adding extra hot water if necessary.

Add the kidney beans and cook for another 20–30 minutes. Stir in the yoghurt, a tablespoonful at a time, tomato purée and the salt. Simmer for 5 minutes. Remove 4 tablespoons of lentils, mash and stir back in.

To make the *tarka*, heat the fats in a non-stick frying pan and sauté the onion over a moderate heat and the remaining ginger until golden, about 7–8 minutes. Add the garlic paste and cook for 1 further minute. Add the tomatoes and cook until pulpy, about 3–4 minutes. Stir the *tarka* into the lentils and cook over a low heat for another 10 minutes, mashing the lentils lightly as you do. Stir in the remaining spices and the coriander. The lentils should be thick and creamy.

white cheese in a creamy tomato sauce
SHAHI PANEER

Although this is one of my all-time favourite paneer dishes, I only recently learned how to make a good (but fattening) version of it. Thanks, SB. Here I have streamlined the spices and replaced the usual cream with milk. The result is a delicate dish with a beautiful mild, slightly sweet, thick gravy, which, although it has all the same spices as a curry, tastes nothing like the stereotypical curried dish. It is so creamy that no one can tell the difference between this and the full-fat version. Sceptical? Try it for yourself.

Serves 4–5

2 tbs vegetable oil
1 medium onion, thinly sliced
½ tsp each turmeric, coriander and red chilli powders
½ tsp garam masala
2 medium tomatoes, cut into wedges
250ml (9 fl oz) hot water
2 fat garlic cloves, grated

3 green chillies, whole
salt to taste
1 tbs tomato purée
200ml (7 fl oz) semi-skimmed milk
300g (10½ oz) low-fat *paneer* (see p. 38), cut into 2.5cm (1 inch) cubes
fresh coriander, chopped, to garnish

Heat the oil in a medium non-stick sauté pan. Add the onion and soften for about 3–4 minutes over a moderate heat without colouring. Add the spices and stir for 30 seconds.

Add the tomatoes and reduce for 5 minutes. Add 100ml (3½ fl oz) of the water and reduce again over a moderate heat.

Add the garlic, chillies, salt and tomato purée, and cook, stirring, for 1 minute. Add the remaining water, bring to the boil and then simmer for 10 minutes. The tomatoes should have completely broken down by now.

Reduce all the excess liquid in the pan. Add the milk and cook for another 5 minutes, stirring often. Add the *paneer* and stir to coat in the sauce. Simmer for 3–4 minutes and serve hot, garnished with the fresh coriander.

potato and pea turnovers
ALOO MATTAR KE SAMOSE

I've watched so many women reluctantly pass over these traditionally fattening snacks for 'safer' nibbles while the men happily tucked in, that I devised this low-fat baked version. Normally samosas are deep-fried and heavy but filo pastry bakes well to produce light and crisp snacks, leaving the filling as the main star. You can fill them with almost any vegetable or meat as long as it is cooked. These small bite-size samosas make perfect appetisers but larger ones can be made for meals. They can be assembled in advance and frozen (only if you are using fresh or chilled filo pastry, not frozen, and fresh peas). Bake from frozen, giving them 25–30 minutes extra cooking time. Serve with *Green Chutney* (p. 184).

Makes 30 small samosas or 15 medium ones

1 packet fresh or frozen filo pastry, thawed

3 tbs melted butter for brushing (optional)

lite cooking spray

FILLING

600g (1 lb 5½ oz) waxy new potatoes

1 level tsp coriander seeds

2 tsp vegetable oil

1–2 green chillies, seeded and sliced (optional)

1½ tsp coriander powder

1 level tsp dried mango powder

100g (3½ oz) shelled fresh green peas or frozen peas, thawed

½ tsp cumin powder

1 level tsp black peppercorns, coarsely crushed

3 tbs chopped fresh coriander

1 tsp salt or to taste

First, make the filling. Boil the potatoes in plenty of water until tender, about 10–15 minutes. Drain, cool slightly and peel. Crush into small lumps with your hands.

Dry-fry the coriander seeds until fragrant and coarsely pound in a pestle and mortar.

Heat the oil in a small non-stick saucepan and fry the chilli (if using), coriander seeds and powdered spices for 30–40 seconds. Add the peas and cumin powder and cook for 5 minutes. Take off the heat and stir in the potatoes, black peppercorns, fresh coriander and salt. Mix well. Allow to cool.

Preheat the oven to 190°C/375°F/Gas 5. Unroll the pastry so that it is flat. Take 3 sheets, and cover the rest with cling film and a damp tea towel. Cut them in half widthways. Then cut each half into 3 even strips to give 6 in total per sheet. Stack and cover with cling film and a damp tea towel. Peel off one strip. Brush with butter or spray evenly with lite cooking spray. Place 1 teaspoon of the cooled filling on one of the short ends, leaving a 2cm (¾ in) border. Take the right corner and fold diagonally to the left, enclosing the filling and forming a triangle. Press down on the pastry to seal. Fold again along the upper crease of the triangle. Keep folding in this way until you reach the end of the strip. Seal well with your fingers. Brush the surface with the butter or spray again. Place on a baking sheet and cover while you make the rest.

Bake in the centre of the preheated oven until golden and crisp, about 15–20 minutes, turning halfway through cooking. Serve hot but not straight from the oven as the filling will be superheated.

traditional pea pilaff
MATTAR PULLAO

This dish is one of the more popular party options. The flavours and textures are well balanced and unobtrusive so that it acts as a suitable foil to everything served with it. Indians prefer fresh peas in the pilaff as frozen ones can be a little sweet, but either are fine. You can make this dish earlier in the day and reheat, covered with a damp tea towel in the microwave.

Serves 6-8
(quantities
can be
halved)

1½ tbs vegetable oil
1 small onion, thinly sliced
175g (6 oz) shelled green peas, fresh
 or frozen
400g (14 oz) Basmati or long-grained
 white rice, washed and soaked for
 30 minutes
salt to taste
750ml (3 cups) hot water
2 tbs lemon juice or to taste

WHOLE SPICES
6 cloves
3 large bay leaves
3 brown cardamom pods
4 green cardamom pods
5cm (2 inch) cinnamon stick, broken
 into a couple of shavings
1½ tsp cumin seeds

Heat the oil in a large non-stick saucepan. Add the onion and gently sauté until golden, about 8–10 minutes. Add the whole spices and cook until fragrant – around 1 minute. Add the peas, rice, salt and water. Taste and adjust the seasoning if necessary for a subtle taste of salt.

Bring to the boil, cover and cook over the lowest heat, undisturbed, for about 12 minutes. There should be no water left and the rice grains should be more or less cooked. Take off the heat and leave covered and undisturbed for another 10 minutes to allow the rice to finish off in the steam. Remove the lid and let any excess moisture evaporate.

Drizzle over the lemon juice and gently mix in with a fork while fluffing up the grains.

These flat-breads are cooked to semi-charred perfection in just 1 minute in restaurant *tandoor* ovens. They are really easy to make and can be grilled, cooked in the oven or in a dry frying pan. Once proved, they are very quick to cook. Vary the recipe with different herbs, spices or adding garlic, finely chopped onion, pepper and sea salt.

charred (nearly) flat-bread
NAAN

**Makes 6
(quantities
can be
doubled)**

250g (9 oz) plain flour
1 tsp each salt and granulated or
   caster sugar
2 tsp fast-action powdered yeast
2 tsp vegetable oil plus extra for
   brushing
3 tbs low-fat yoghurt, beaten

1 small egg, beaten
water to bind (around 80–100ml/
   4–5 tbs)
1 good pinch of nigella (onion) or
   poppy or cumin or sesame seeds, or
   a mixture of them all (optional)

Sift the dry ingredients (except the seeds, if using) into a bowl. Make a well in the centre and pour in the oil, yoghurt and egg. Mix and slowly add the water until you have a soft, pliable dough. Knead well for 8–10 minutes. Place in a large oiled bowl, cover with cling film and a plate; prove in a warm place until doubled in size, about 1 hour, or longer in the fridge.

Heat a non-stick frying or griddle pan or preheat the oven to its highest setting and place a baking sheet to preheat on one of the upper shelves.

Divide the dough into 6 pieces; take a piece and cover the rest. Lightly flour your work surface and roll the dough into a thin circle or oval, about 3–4mm (⅛ inch) thick. Brush on a little oil. If cooking in a pan slap it onto the hot surface and sprinkle over a good pinch of seeds (if using). Cook for 1 minute, then turn and cook the underside until brown spots appear. Lower the heat and turn the bread. Cook for another 20–30 seconds or so until there are a few spots where the *naan* has charred and it is completely cooked. This whole process should take about 2–3 minutes.

If using the oven, place the bread on the preheated baking sheet. Bake until puffed up, about 1 minute each side, turning halfway through cooking, and then finish under the grill until lightly charred.

BY NOW MOST of us know that the word 'curry' is more English than Indian. However, everyday usage has pushed it firmly into the Anglo-Indian lexicon. We now call most gravied dishes a 'curry'. This is not a very accurate description as the gravy could be based on tomatoes, onions, coconut, yoghurt or a combination of them all, and it does not really tell us much about the actual curry. What we really mean is any dish with a lot of gravy. This chapter contains a variety of recipes with plenty of gravy, based on classic Indian dishes.

CURRY FLAVOUR ...

Apart from the obvious mouth-watering taste and the layers of flavours, curries have many virtues. For a start, they are actually very good for you. The basic ingredients used are known to possess many healthful properties: antioxidant, antibacterial and even anti-inflammatory. Curries are very versatile and you can add any ingredient to the basic sauce as it goes with everything. Another boon is that, like us, the dishes improve with a day's rest, so make your chosen curry 24 hours in advance and reheat it the following day when you get home from work.

As there is no 'curry' dish in India, you can be sure that there is no 'curry' spice. The aroma and flavours that you get from freshly ground spices are unbeatable. It is like comparing fresh and dried herbs. Yes, you will get some of the original flavour in a 'curry' spice but if you had the choice, which would you choose? And unlike fresh herbs, whole spices keep very well when properly stored and are not at all expensive. If it is problematic to buy the whole seeds, at least buy individual spices so that you can tailor the dishes to your individual taste.

The best tip I can give you in this chapter is to take the time to make a good curry base. The most useful ingredient in my life is my low-fat *Everyday Curry Paste* (p. 28). Make up a large batch and store it in the fridge or freezer, so all you have to do is spoon some out whenever necessary. Once you start to use it you will never look back.

northern fish curry
THARRI WALI MACHCHI

Each region has its own version of fish curry. This is based on an old family recipe using freshwater fish. My father prides himself on this dish which he considers to be his father's recipe, although I have yet to see him pick up a stirring spoon. Use any firm-fleshed and robust white fish that won't disintegrate during cooking. As Indians like to eat with our fingers, I often use fish steaks, but if you find the bones a bother, buy thick-cut fillets instead.

Serves 2
(quantities
can be
doubled)

2 tsp vegetable oil
1 bay leaf
½ tsp brown mustard seeds, ground in a pestle and mortar
1 small blade of mace
1 tsp garlic paste (optional)
2–3 rounded tbs *Everyday Curry Paste* (p. 28)
2 good pinches of chilli powder
salt to taste
400ml (13 fl oz) hot water

1 tsp rice flour, dissolved in 2 tbs water
175g (6 oz) firm white fish fillets or steaks, cut into 4cm (1½ inch) pieces
2 good pinches each of dried mango powder and freshly ground black pepper
½ tsp garam masala
a handful of chopped fresh coriander (leaves and stalks)

Heat the oil in a large non-stick saucepan and fry the bay leaf, mustard seeds and mace for 30 seconds. Add the garlic paste (if using) and cook for another 30 seconds. Add the curry paste, chilli, salt and 100ml (3½ fl oz) of the water, and cook until reduced, 5–7 minutes.

Add the remaining water, bring to the boil and simmer for 2–3 minutes. Add the rice flour and stir until the curry thickens. Add the fish, cover and simmer on a low heat until just cooked through, about 5–8 minutes depending on the fish.

Add the remaining spices, and taste to adjust the seasoning. Be careful not to break up the fish. Add extra water from the kettle if you want more gravy. Stir in the coriander and serve hot.

A classic homey chicken curry that is made all over north India. It is quite distinct from the creamy curries seen in Western restaurants and, to my palate, much tastier. The flavours are bold but in perfect harmony. This dish has a depth that belies its minimal fat content, and it leaves you feeling light, infinitely satisfied and waiting for the next instalment.

classic chicken curry
THARRI WALA MURGH

Serves 3–4 (quantities can be doubled)

1 tbs vegetable oil
1 medium onion, chopped
1 bay leaf
1 blade of mace
½ tsp cumin seeds
1 tbs garlic paste
1 tsp ginger paste
1–2 green chillies, chopped or left whole
½ tsp turmeric powder
1½ tsp coriander powder

salt to taste
1 medium tomato, grated
450ml (15 fl oz) hot water
450g (1 lb) chicken joints, skinned, rinsed and all visible fat removed
1 tsp low-fat yoghurt, beaten
½ tsp each garam masala
1 good tsp dried fenugreek leaves, crumbled
a handful of chopped fresh coriander

Heat the oil in a large non-stick saucepan. Add the onion and gently cook until golden brown, about 10 minutes. Add the bay leaf, mace and cumin seeds and stir until fragrant, about 30 seconds. Add the garlic and ginger pastes and the chilli, and cook gently for 1 minute, then stir in the turmeric, coriander powder and salt. Add 100ml (3½ fl oz) of the water and the tomato, turn up the heat and reduce until thick.

Add the chicken, turn up the heat and toss in the pan for 3–4 minutes until the edges turn white. Cover and cook on a low heat for 10 minutes, stirring occasionally. Then stir in the remaining 350ml (11½ fl oz) water, bring to the boil and simmer, covered, on a low heat until the chicken joints have cooked through, around 15–25 minutes, depending on their size.

Once the chicken is tender, stir in the yoghurt and cook for 4 minutes, tossing the meat in the gravy. Add extra water from the kettle if necessary; the gravy should have the consistency of single cream. Stir in the remaining spices and fresh coriander, taste and adjust the seasoning. Serve hot.

cheat's quick chicken curry
JHATTPATTA THARRI WALA MURGH

This dish is not a poor relative of the previous recipe but it is the quick version if you already have *Everyday Curry Paste* (p. 28) in the fridge. Garlicky and rich in chilli, it is absolutely delicious. Green chilli does add an extra flavour but you can use chilli powder instead. I often make this so that I will have leftovers for *Chicken Biryani* (p. 169), an all-in-one chicken and rice dish.

Serves 2–3
(quantities
can be
doubled)

2 tsp vegetable oil
300g (10½ oz) chicken joints, skinned,
   rinsed and all visible fat removed
1 tsp garlic paste
1 green chilli, left whole, and/or
   2 good pinches of chilli powder
1 tsp coriander powder
2 rounded tbs *Everyday Curry Paste*
   (p. 28)

150ml (5 fl oz) hot water
salt to taste
1 generous tbs low-fat yoghurt, beaten
1 tsp dried fenugreek leaves,
   crumbled
½ tsp garam masala
a handful of chopped fresh coriander
   (leaves and stalks)

Heat the oil in a non-stick saucepan until quite hot. Add the chicken and sear well for about 4–5 minutes. Lower the heat, add the garlic paste and chilli and cook for 1 minute. Add the coriander powder, curry paste, water and salt. Stir and bring to the boil. Then cover and cook on a low heat until the chicken is done, about 20–30 minutes, depending on the size of the joints. Stir occasionally and add a splash of hot water if necessary.

Once the chicken is tender, stir in the yoghurt and toss the chicken in the gravy for about 5 minutes. Add extra water from the kettle for a thick gravy. Stir in the fenugreek, garam masala and fresh coriander, taste and adjust the seasoning, and serve hot.

chicken in spinach gravy
SAAG WALA MURGH

The sneaky addition of puréed spinach which just melts into the savoury and not too spicy gravy makes this dish the ultimate candidate for inclusion in my life. The puréed spinach adds creaminess and body to the gravy without the use of any fattening ingredients. A great way to get children to eat their greens, not to mention certain adults. A pregnant friend of mine couldn't face vegetables but lapped up the greens in this sauce. I often use frozen puréed spinach but fresh is more than welcome.

700g (1 lb 8 oz) chicken joints, skinned, rinsed and all visible fat removed

450g (1 lb) frozen spinach, thawed, or fresh spinach, picked over and washed in at least three changes of water

½ tsp salt

1½ tsp each of unsalted butter and vegetable oil

1 medium onion, finely chopped

1 tsp cumin seeds

2 tsp garlic, chopped

2 tsp fresh ginger, chopped

1–2 green chillies, seeded and finely sliced (optional)

1 level tsp garam masala

1 tbs lemon juice or to taste

MARINADE

4 tbs low-fat yoghurt, beaten

½ tsp garam masala

1 tsp each of garlic and ginger pastes

2 tsp coriander powder

Serves 4

Combine the ingredients for the marinade in a non-metallic bowl. Add the chicken, mix well and marinate for as long as possible, preferably overnight, in the fridge. Bring back to room temperature.

Place the spinach in a pan with the salt. Cook for 5 minutes if using frozen spinach and 10 minutes if using fresh. Drain well. Cool slightly and purée in a food processor. If you don't have one, pass it through a mouli. Set aside.

Heat the butter and oil in a large non-stick saucepan and fry the onion until browned, lowering the heat once it starts to colour, about 10–12 minutes. Stir often. Add the cumin seeds and cook until fragrant, about 30 seconds.

Add the garlic, ginger and chilli (if using), and stir-fry for 1 minute over a low heat. Increase the heat, add the chicken (reserving the marinade) and toss in the pan to brown all over, around 3–4 minutes.

Add 2 tablespoons of water to the marinade, stir well and pour into the pan, together with the spinach and salt to taste. Bring to the boil, then cook, covered, over a moderate heat, stirring occasionally, until the chicken has cooked through, about 20–30 minutes, depending on the size of the joints.

Uncover the pan and dry off the excess water released by the spinach over a high heat. Stir in the garam masala and lemon juice and serve hot.

This comforting, one-pot meat and potato curry is perfect for a cold winter evening. The combination of the buttery potatoes and tender, flavourful lamb is brought alive by the heady spices, making this classic dish a family favourite. Whole spices really lift this curry but as an alternative you can stir in 1 scant teaspoon of garam masala before serving.

lamb and potato curry
ALOO GOSHT

2 tbs vegetable oil

500g (1 lb 2 oz) lean lamb, cubed, rinsed and patted dry

1–2 green chillies, seeded and finely chopped (optional)

2 tsp each of ginger and garlic pastes

4–5 tbs *Everyday Curry Paste* (p. 28)

salt to taste

650ml (22 fl oz) hot water

2 medium potatoes, peeled and quartered

1 rounded tsp dried fenugreek leaves, crumbled

¼–½ tsp garam masala

a good handful of chopped fresh coriander (leaves and stalks)

juice of ½ lemon or to taste

WHOLE SPICES

3 each black and green cardamom pods, lightly crushed

4 cloves

4cm (1½ inch) cinnamon stick, lightly broken

3 small bay leaves

1 blade of mace

Serves 4

Heat the oil in a large, heavy-based, non-stick pan, and sear the lamb over a high heat along with the chilli (if using) for about 4–5 minutes, until well browned.

Add the whole spices and ginger and garlic pastes and cook for 1 minute over a moderate heat. Stir in the curry paste, salt and 150ml (5 fl oz) of the water. Bring to the boil, cover and cook on a low heat for about 50 minutes, adding 250ml (9 fl oz) of the water after 10 minutes. Stir in extra water if necessary.

Add the potatoes and the remaining water, bring to the boil and then simmer, covered, until both lamb and potatoes are tender, another 20–25 minutes or so. Stir occasionally and add a splash of hot water if necessary.

Uncover, turn up the heat and toss the meat in the gravy, reducing it to a good thick consistency. Stir in the remaining spices, coriander and lemon juice to taste. Cook for a further minute and serve hot.

quorn *or* vegetarian chunky curry
THARRI WALE QUORN

This curry is the vegetarian alternative to a chicken curry and is every bit as good. Quorn is a low-fat, vegetarian protein with the character of chicken. It is only available in the UK at present but will hopefully find its way to other countries. If you are a demi-vegetarian this is the dish that will push you over the line. If you can't get hold of quorn, substitute with vegetarian protein chunks.

Serves 4

1½ tbs vegetable oil
1 tsp ginger paste
1 heaped tsp garlic paste
1–2 green chillies, seeded and sliced, or left whole
1 tsp coriander powder
salt to taste
4 tbs *Everyday Curry Paste* (p. 28)
1 small tomato, ground or grated
1 tbs ground almonds

350g (12 oz) quorn or vegetarian protein chunks
400ml (13 fl oz) hot water
2 tbs low-fat yoghurt, beaten
1 rounded tsp dried fenugreek leaves, crumbled
½ tsp each garam masala and cumin powder
a handful of chopped fresh coriander (leaves and stalks)

Heat the oil in a large non-stick saucepan, add the ginger and garlic pastes and chilli and fry for 30 seconds. Stir in the coriander powder and salt. Add the curry paste, tomato, ground almonds and a splash of water. Cook on a moderate heat for 5 minutes.

Add the quorn and the water, stir, bring to the boil and then simmer, covered, for 10 minutes. Uncover, add more water from the kettle if necessary, and then stir in the yoghurt, a tablespoonful at a time.

Stir in the remaining spices and fresh coriander, and serve hot.

egg curry
THARRI WALE ANDAY

A fabulous curry that is great for both vegetarians and meat-eaters. The flavours are indescribable; the combination of eggs and spices is a match made in culinary heaven. Just give it a try. Use any leftovers in a kedgeree or a rice pilaff.

Serves 4
(quantities
can be
doubled)

1 tbs vegetable oil
½ small onion, finely chopped
½ tsp garlic paste
½ tsp ginger paste
1 green chilli, left whole or chopped
  for added heat (optional)
1 tsp coriander powder
½ tsp turmeric powder
1–2 good pinches of red chilli powder
salt to taste
2 small tomatoes, ground or grated

250ml (9 fl oz) hot water
3 eggs, hard-boiled (about 8 minutes
  in boiling water) and halved
  lengthways
½ tsp garam masala
freshly ground black pepper to taste
1 tsp dried fenugreek leaves,
  crumbled
a handful of chopped fresh coriander
  (leaves and stalks)

Heat the oil in a small non-stick saucepan and gently fry the onion until golden, 5–6 minutes. Add the garlic and ginger pastes, green chilli (if using), coriander powder, turmeric, red chilli powder and salt. Follow with the tomatoes and cook on a high heat for 5 minutes.

Add the water and bring to the boil. Add the egg halves and simmer gently for 10 minutes. Carefully stir in the remaining spices and fresh coriander and serve hot.

Egg Curry shown with Quick Vegetable Pilaff

chickpea curry
THARRI WALE CHOLLE

This dish is earthy and the spices are warm rather than strong. It is really quick and easy to make. Although dried and soaked chickpeas produce a better dish than the canned variety, to be honest I can't remember the last time I made this dish from scratch. *Channa masala* is a spice mix specially blended to enhance the taste of chickpeas and is one of those secrets of authentic home cooking that you normally never hear about. Buy it in Indian stores; it keeps well and is definitely worth the money. Add extra chilli if you like the heat, or for an authentic twist add a few sliced mushrooms cooked in the hot oil.

Serves 3 (quantities can be doubled)

1 tbs vegetable oil
½ tsp cumin seeds
1 tsp fresh ginger, chopped
½ tsp garlic, chopped
½ tsp turmeric powder
½ tsp coriander powder
1 medium tomato, ground
1 rounded tbs *Everyday Curry Paste* (p. 28)
200ml (7 fl oz) hot water

400g (14 oz) can of chickpeas, drained and washed, or 150g (5 oz) dried chickpeas, soaked overnight and cooked as directed on p. 22
1½ tsp *channa masala*
2 good pinches each of garam masala, chilli powder, freshly ground black pepper and roasted cumin powder
salt to taste
a handful of chopped fresh coriander (leaves and stalks)

Heat the oil in a small non-stick saucepan, add the cumin and cook for 30 seconds. Then stir in the ginger, garlic, turmeric and coriander powder and cook for 30 seconds. Add the tomato, curry paste and water. Bring to the boil for 2–3 minutes.

Add the chickpeas, cover, lower the heat and simmer for 6 minutes. Remove 2 tablespoons of chickpeas, mash and stir back into the pan, adding the remaining ingredients. Serve hot. This curry thickens as it cools.

This curry is light, pleasantly tart and bursting with interesting flavours. If you prefer, you can leave out the fried dumplings or substitute 250g (9 oz) of your favourite vegetables.

yoghurt curry
KADDI

YOGHURT CURRY
3 rounded tbs gram flour (*besan*)
250ml (9 fl oz) low-fat soured yoghurt
  (leave out overnight to sour)
750ml (25 fl oz) cold water
½ tsp turmeric powder
1½ tsp salt
1 tbs vegetable oil
½ medium onion, sliced
1 tsp brown mustard seeds
½ tsp each of cumin and fenugreek seeds
around 10 fresh or dried curry leaves
1–3 small dry red chillies or
  ¼–½ tsp red chilli powder
lemon juice to taste

DUMPLINGS
60g (2 oz) gram flour (*besan*), sifted
about 6 tbs cold water
½ small onion, finely chopped
1 green chilli, finely chopped
½ tsp salt
a handful of baby spinach leaves,
  shredded
oil for frying

Whisk the flour into the yoghurt till lump-free, then whisk in the water, turmeric and salt. Set aside.

Heat the oil in a non-stick saucepan. Add the onion and gently cook till just soft and just turning golden, about 8 minutes. Add the seeds, curry leaves and chillies, and stir for about 30–40 seconds.

Add the yoghurt mixture and bring to the boil, stirring. Lower the heat and simmer for 30 minutes (leave the wooden spoon in the curry as it cooks, the old wives say; this will stop the yoghurt from curdling, and who are we to argue). Stir occasionally.

Meanwhile, whisk together all the ingredients for the dumplings. Heat enough oil for deep-fat frying to about 180°C/350°F. Drop in teaspoonfuls and fry until golden, about 2–3 minutes. Drain on kitchen paper and add to the curry. Simmer for 5 minutes. The curry should have the consistency of creamy soup. Add lemon juice to taste and serve hot.

WHEN YOU'RE JUGGLING children, a job and a partner, cooking from scratch may not seem realistic. We spend more than ever on convenient takeaways and processed meals. As a result, children are heavier than they have ever been before. It's a *Catch 22* situation: you want to feed your children the best and freshest foods, but are too busy working and getting their lives organised to have any free time left to cook properly. But nothing beats a home-cooked meal; you control what goes in it, so there are no artificial flavours, colours or preservatives and it is made exactly as you would like.

QUICK FAMILY MEALS

That a fresh, home-cooked meal is preferable to a store-bought one is fact. What is less obvious is what should be included in this chapter. In hindsight, I realise my formative years included the seasoning of my tastebuds due to a curiosity towards food and an inherent gluttony gene. I ate everything on my plate. There was not a trace of the fussy eater in me. Consequently, I have always found it difficult to understand the plight of much-suffering parents, tortured by junk-food-loving children. I do try to empathise.

I do believe this is the age when you should be introducing new flavours to the impressionable young. Start them off on their culinary excursions, even if it is under the guise of familiar looking territory. The recipes in this chapter pair familiar ingredients with new flavours and are easy to make thus minimising your time in the kitchen. Where possible, I use frozen or store-cupboard ingredients for convenience. Using unusual ingredients in familiar dishes is a sneaky way to get children trying new flavours.

For best results, marinate the chicken pieces in the morning or the night before. Then all you have to do is throw the whole thing in a pan and it practically cooks itself.

cumin-scented chicken
JEERA MURGH

700g (1 lb 8 oz) chicken joints, skinned, rinsed and all visible fat removed

1 tsp butter

2 tsp vegetable oil

salt to taste

½ tsp garam masala

lemon juice to taste

a handful of chopped fresh coriander (leaves and stalks)

Serves 4-5

MARINADE

1 rounded tbs cumin seeds, coarsely pounded in a pestle and mortar

1 rounded tbs garlic paste

1 level tsp ginger paste

2 tsp coriander powder

1–2 green chillies, seeded and sliced or left whole (optional)

½ tsp each garam masala and freshly ground black pepper

1 chicken stock cube, dissolved in 3 tbs hot water

2 generous tbs low-fat yoghurt, beaten

Combine all the ingredients for the marinade and place in a non-metallic bowl or plastic freezer bag. Prick the chicken all over and coat well with the marinade. Leave for as long as possible, preferably overnight, in the fridge. Bring back to room temperature.

Melt the butter and oil in a non-stick saucepan; add the chicken (reserving the marinade) and sear evenly all over, about 3–4 minutes. Add a splash of water from the kettle to the marinade, swirl around and pour into the pan.

Add a little salt, cover and cook over a low heat until the chicken is done, about 25–35 minutes, depending on the size of the joints. Stir occasionally, adding extra water if necessary.

Once the chicken is cooked, increase the heat and reduce the gravy to a very thick sauce so that it clings to the meat, tossing constantly for 3–4 minutes. Taste and adjust the seasoning if necessary. Stir in the garam masala, lemon juice and fresh coriander, and serve hot.

Mangalore is known for its coconut-flavoured seafood dishes but as they are usually high in fat, I have kept the added fat to a minimum. You can use any firm sea-water fish; freshwater fish can be a little sweet. You will need a food processor or blender for this dish.

mangalorian fish curry
MANGALORI MACHCHI

1 tsp vegetable oil
½ small onion, finely sliced
2 small tomatoes, each cut into
    8 sections
½ tsp ginger paste
1 green chilli, left whole
1 tsp paprika
salt to taste
½ tsp turmeric
5 tbs coconut milk powder
150ml (5 fl oz) hot water
25g (¾ oz) block of tamarind, soaked
    and juice extracted (see p. 27)
    or to taste

Serves 4-5

2–3 large fish steaks, cut into
    4–6 portions

PASTE
½ small onion, roughly chopped
3 fat garlic cloves
2.5cm (1 inch) piece of fresh ginger,
    peeled
½ tsp cumin seeds
1 good pinch each of brown mustard
    seeds and black peppercorns
1½ tbs coriander seeds or powder
2–3 large mild red chillies, seeded and
    roughly chopped
100ml (3½ fl oz) hot water

First, make the paste. Put all the paste ingredients except the water into a blender or food processor, and process, adding the water slowly, until you have a very fine and fluffy paste. Set aside.

Heat the oil in a large non-stick saucepan and fry the onion for 1 minute. Add the tomatoes, ginger paste, chilli, paprika, salt and turmeric. Stir-fry for 2 minutes. Add the paste and cook, covered, over a moderate heat for 10–12 minutes.

Add the coconut powder together with the water. Bring to the boil and then simmer for 5 minutes. Add the tamarind juice to taste.

Add the fish and swirl the pan to coat it thoroughly. Cook at a moderate to high heat for 5–6 minutes or until the fish is done. Adjust the seasoning and liquid content. The gravy should be creamy but not thick.

chicken with dried pomegranate
ANARDHANA WALA MURGH

Pomegranate may seem a strange combination with chicken, but once dried these jewel-like seeds morph to resemble dark peppercorns but without the heat. This exotic ingredient adds a delicious tang to this savoury dish that is difficult to mimic with anything else. You can find dried pomegranate seeds in any Indian shop, or you can use the powder.

700g (1 lb 8 oz) chicken joints, skinned, rinsed and all visible fat removed
1 tbs vegetable oil
salt to taste
½ tsp garam masala
a handful of chopped fresh coriander (leaves and stalks)
1 tsp lemon juice or to taste

Serves 4-5

MARINADE
1½ tbs dried pomegranate powder or seeds, roasted for 1–2 minutes and ground
1 heaped tbs garlic paste
1 level tbs ginger paste
2 level tsp coriander powder
½ tsp garam masala
1–2 green chillies, seeded and sliced (optional)

Prick the chicken all over with a fork. Combine all the ingredients for the marinade and place in a non-metallic bowl or plastic freezer bag. Rub into the chicken and marinate for as long as possible, preferably overnight, in the fridge. Bring back to room temperature.

Heat the oil in a non-stick saucepan. Scrape the chicken and the marinade into the pan and brown all over on a moderate to high heat for about 3–4 minutes.

Add the salt and a splash of water from the kettle. Cover and cook over a low heat until the chicken has cooked through, about 25–35 minutes, depending on the size of the joints. Stir occasionally, adding splashes of hot water whenever the pan seems dry.

Once the chicken is cooked, uncover the pan, increase the heat and toss in the gravy for 5 minutes, adding more water or reducing excess liquid, as necessary. This intensifies the flavours. Taste and adjust the seasoning. Stir in the garam masala, fresh coriander and lemon juice, if necessary, and serve hot.

I used to delight in helping my mother make this hands-on dish when I was a child, standing on a stool at the hob and trying to shape round, firm meatballs in my palms. This is real comfort food. Children love meatballs and this dish is no exception; if you wish, you can leave out the chillies and serve with buttered egg noodles for a more familiar plate.

meatball curry
THARRI WALE KOFTE

MEATBALLS
300g (10½ oz) lean minced lamb
1 tsp fresh ginger, chopped
1 green chilli, seeded and chopped
    (optional)
1 tbs chopped fresh coriander
1 tsp salt
½ tsp white wine vinegar

CURRY
1 tbs vegetable oil
1–2 green chillies, left whole or
    chopped

1 tsp garlic, chopped
½ tsp coriander powder
4 tbs *Everyday Curry Paste* (p. 28)
    or to taste
400ml (13 fl oz) hot water
1 generous tbs low-fat yoghurt, beaten
½ tsp garam masala
1 tsp dried fenugreek leaves,
    crumbled
a small handful of chopped fresh
    coriander (leaves and stalks)

Serves 4 with other dishes

Mix together the ingredients for the meatballs. Form small handfuls into tight, walnut-sized portions and set aside.

Next, make the curry. Heat the oil in a non-stick saucepan and add the chillies and garlic and cook for 30–40 seconds. Add the coriander powder, curry paste and water, bring to the boil and simmer for 5 minutes. Stir in the yoghurt.

Carefully drop the meatballs into the curry one by one. Bring back to the boil, cover and cook over a low heat for a further 7–10 minutes or until the meatballs are cooked through. Do not stir too often once you have added the meatballs.

Stir in the garam masala, fenugreek leaves and fresh coriander, cook for 1 further minute and serve.

yoghurt-simmered fish

DAHI WALI MACHCHI

This dish is flavourful and spicy, yet the yoghurt tames it, giving the fish a delicate and subtle (by Indian standards) flavour. This is an ideal dish for those not yet initiated into the world of these robust spices. You can make the gravy in advance and then simmer the fish just before you are ready to eat. Any white fish fillets can be used in this dish; I suggest sole or halibut as they both have a delicate flavour that works well. Serve with plain boiled rice.

1½ tbs vegetable oil

1 large onion, finely chopped

2 green chillies, left whole

2 tsp garlic paste

1 rounded tsp ginger paste

salt to taste

½ tsp turmeric powder

2 tsp coriander powder

180ml (6 fl oz) low-fat yoghurt, beaten

25g (¾ oz) almonds, blanched, skinned and ground or bought ground almonds

1 medium tomato, cut into large pieces

150ml (5 fl oz) hot water

175g (6 oz) fillets of sole, halibut or haddock, cleaned

freshly ground black pepper to taste

½ tsp garam masala

a handful of chopped fresh coriander (leaves and stalks)

Serves 4

Heat the oil in a large non-stick frying pan. Add the onion and gently fry until golden and shrivelled, about 10 minutes, turning the heat down after it starts to colour. Add the chillies, garlic and ginger pastes and cook for 30 seconds. Add the salt, turmeric and coriander powders and stir for another 30 seconds. Add the yoghurt, a tablespoonful at a time, and stir to incorporate. Add a splash of hot water. Simmer over a moderate heat for 10 minutes. If the yoghurt looks grainy, do not worry; turn the heat up, stir well and it will come back together.

Add the almonds and tomato, and cook until softened, about 6 minutes, adding splashes of hot water whenever the pan starts to dry out.

Stir in the water and bring to the boil. Add the fish, preferably skin side down as this helps keep it together. Turn down the heat, cover and simmer until the fish is tender, about 4 minutes for sole, 7–8 minutes for halibut, depending on thickness, and 5–6 minutes for haddock. Turn halfway through cooking. The gravy should be thick but not clinging to the fish. If the gravy seems too watery, remove the fish and reduce it until you have the right consistency. Then return the fish to the pan.

Taste and adjust the seasoning. Sprinkle over the black pepper, garam masala and fresh coriander and serve.

white cheese in spinach
PAALAK PANEER

Paneer, a home-made unsalted cheese, has a freshness that offsets this perfectly spiced creamy spinach purée. This dish is a great way to inject a healthy dose of calcium and greens into children's diets while disguising the taste of the spinach. I prefer fresh spinach as it has a smoother texture but you can use frozen. I also leave the cheese 'raw' but if you wish it can be deep-fried or baked. You will need a food processor or blender for this dish.

800g (1 lb 9 oz) spinach, picked over and washed or frozen spinach, thawed and chopped
1 tbs vegetable oil
1 medium onion, finely chopped
5cm (2 inch) piece of fresh ginger, peeled and cut into fine shreds
1 rounded tsp garlic, chopped
1–2 green chillies, halved lengthways (optional)
1 tsp coriander powder
1 medium tomato, ground or grated

salt to taste
3 generous tbs low-fat yoghurt, beaten
250ml (9 fl oz) hot water
200g (7 oz) low-fat *paneer*, cubed, made from 1.8 litres (3 pints) milk (p. 38)
a knob of unsalted butter
1 tsp dried fenugreek leaves, crumbled
½ tsp garam masala
lemon juice to taste

Serves 4

If using fresh spinach, wilt in a saucepan with a splash of water for about 3–4 minutes, or heat through the frozen spinach. Reduce most of the excess liquid, drain and blend in a food processor or with a hand blender to a fine paste. Set aside.

Heat the oil in a non-stick saucepan and gently fry the onion until golden, about 10 minutes. On a low heat, add the ginger, garlic and chilli (if using) and stir-fry for 30 seconds. Then stir in the coriander powder. Follow with the tomato and salt and reduce over a moderate heat until pulpy.

Mix in the spinach and cook at a moderate heat for 5 minutes. Add the yoghurt, a tablespoonful at a time, stirring between additions. Add the water to loosen the curry; it should have a smooth, creamy consistency. Spoon in the *paneer* and heat through for 4–5 minutes. Finally stir in the butter, fenugreek leaves and garam masala. Taste, adjust the seasoning and add lemon juice as necessary. Serve hot.

potatoes with onions and mustard seeds
ALOO MASALA

These delicious, easy-cook potatoes are normally rolled in large *Rice and Lentil Pancakes* (p. 164) to make one of the most popular dishes in Tamil Nadu, the southernmost state in India. This is served with *Vegetable and Lentil Curry* (p. 144) and *Quick Coconut Chutney* (p. 185). You can buy the batter mix for these pancakes from Indian stores or just follow the recipe in the book. Alternatively serve with rice or *roti* (p. 34) for an equally delicious meal.

Serves 4

500g (1 lb 2 oz) waxy new potatoes, boiled or microwaved until tender and peeled
2 tbs vegetable oil
1 rounded tsp brown mustard seeds
2–3 small, dried red chillies, lightly crushed

15 fresh or dried curry leaves
1 medium onion, sliced
½ tsp turmeric powder
2 tsp coriander powder
salt to taste
½ tsp dried mango powder
1–2 tsp lemon juice or to taste

Crush the cooked potatoes in your hands to make large uneven lumps. Set aside.

Heat the oil in a non-stick frying pan. Add the mustard seeds, chillies and curry leaves (take care as the seeds will splutter) and cook for about 20 seconds. Add the onion and gently sauté until soft and just golden, about 10 minutes.

Stir in the turmeric, coriander and salt to taste. Add the potatoes and sauté for 3–4 minutes, adding a splash of hot water if necessary. The potatoes should be moist but not wet. Stir in the dried mango powder and lemon juice and serve hot.

butternut squash with fennel
SITAPHAL

Anyone who has tried this dish swears that from then onwards it is the only way they enjoy squash. It is fragrant rather than hot and the hint of sugar enhances the vegetable's natural sweetness, but diehard chilli fans can add extra zing with a spoon of pickle or fresh green chillies. In India they would use standard orange pumpkin but I prefer butternut or kambocha squashes to orange pumpkin, as they are less fibrous and have a creamier flavour. All the effort lies in cutting up the squash rather than the actual cooking. It is so easy and absolutely delicious.

Serves 4-6

1 (around 800g/1 lb 9 oz) small butternut or kambocha squash or pumpkin
2 tsp vegetable oil
½ tsp fenugreek seeds
½ tsp turmeric powder
1 pinch of red chilli powder
½ tsp coriander powder

½ tsp salt or to taste
150ml (5 fl oz) hot water
½–1 tsp caster or granulated sugar or to taste
1 tsp fennel seeds, well pounded in a pestle and mortar
½ tsp black peppercorns, crushed
½ tsp dried mango powder

Cut the squash into large wedges. Scoop out the seeds and carefully peel off the skin. Cut the flesh into even 2cm (¾ inch) pieces.

Heat the oil in a non-stick saucepan. Add the fenugreek seeds and brown lightly for 20 seconds. Stir in the turmeric, chilli and coriander powders and the salt. Add the squash and the water and mix well.

Bring to the boil, then lower the heat, cover and cook until tender, about 10–13 minutes. Stir occasionally, adding a splash of hot water if necessary.

Uncover the pan and stir in the sugar, fennel seeds, black pepper and dried mango powder. Continue cooking to dry up any excess liquid in the pan. The squash will start to break down at the edges and the dish will resemble a lumpy purée. It should be moist but not wet. Serve hot.

layered flat-bread
LACHCHE WALA PARANTHA

This is definitely my favourite Indian bread. It is the layers that form in the rolling process that give it an added lightness and tender flakiness. These flat-breads are easier to make than they seem and so delicious that they are regularly eaten at breakfast, lunch and dinner, taken on long journeys and, just as often, served in fancy restaurants. Serve them with your meal, or with your favourite pickle, or eat them just as they are. If you want to ring the changes, add just *one* optional flavouring to the basic recipe. The bread is also good made with milk rather than water with the added bonus of hidden calcium.

Makes 8 small breads

BASIC RECIPE
200g (7 oz) chapatti flour, or a mix of
    half plain and half wholemeal flour
1 tsp salt
4 tbs melted butter
75–100ml (2½–3½ fl oz) or more water
    or milk, at room temperature
extra flour, for rolling

vegetable oil, for cooking

**OPTIONAL AND HIGHLY RECOMMENDED
    FLAVOURINGS**
dried mint leaves – ½ tsp per bread
carom seeds – ½ tsp per bread
freshly ground black pepper – 1 good
    pinch per bread

Put the flour and salt into a large bowl and rub in half the melted butter until crumbly. Slowly stir in enough water or milk to make a soft dough. It will be wet at first. Knead it for 7–8 minutes, after which it will firm up. Divide the dough into 8 balls, cover with damp kitchen paper and leave to rest for 20 minutes.

Take one piece at a time. Flatten and dip each side in the flour. Roll out into a circle as thin as you can. Spread half a teaspoon of the melted butter over the surface and evenly sprinkle with your chosen flavourings (if using). Taking the side furthest away, roll the dough tightly towards you as you would a swiss roll so that you are left with a long tube. Coil this around itself like a rope and flatten again. Dip in flour again and roll into a large thin round (13cm/5 inches) as you would a normal *roti* (the thinner the better). Repeat with the remaining dough and layer under a damp tea towel to stop them drying out.

Preheat the oven to 200°C/400°F/Gas 6. Heat a flat cast-iron griddle or frying pan until hot. Drizzle the surface with a quarter-teaspoon of oil. Slap the dough on to the surface and reduce the heat to moderate. Cook for 30 seconds, then drizzle half a teaspoon of oil over the uppermost surface of the bread and spread with the back of a spoon. Turn the bread and cook the underside until dark spots appear. Drizzle this side with another half-teaspoon of the oil and turn again. Cook until large brown spots have appeared on both sides. The whole process takes 2–3 minutes. Move the bread in the pan as it cooks so that no one area gets too exposed to the hot spots.

Cover the cooked bread with a tea towel. Repeat with the remaining breads and reheat, if necessary, wrapped in foil, in the preheated oven. Serve hot, warm or at room temperature.

LEGUMES OR PULSES are considered one of nature's great health-foods as they are packed with vitamins and minerals, contain both protein and carbohydrate and are a good source of soluble fibre. It is no wonder, therefore, that they are such an important ingredient in the Indian diet; in fact, the phrase *dal roti*, literally 'lentils and bread', also means a meal.

Pulses are extremely versatile; we soak and grind them, roast them, fry them, simmer them in spiced curries and use their flour in batters and breads to flavour, bind and thicken dishes. They can be eaten with any meal and feature in both sweet and savoury dishes. In the North, they are most often made into robust, earthy curries, which are then scooped up in little conical morsels of flatbread. In the South, lentil curries are thinner so that they can soak through the mound of rice that is served with them.

FINGER ON THE **PULSE**

There seem to be so many rules connected with cooking pulses, but I feel this is a little undeserved; lentils, beans and peas practically cook themselves; see the general instructions on p. 22. As a bonus they are inherently flavoured, so they need very few additions to create delicious dishes.

The West is only just beginning to explore the bounty of pulses that we have been enjoying in the East. As a result, many can still only be found in Indian shops and even these may have more than one name. To add to this confusion, pulses are sold whole or split and with their skins either on or washed off. Until you are familiar with the different varieties, take the Indian name with you and ask for help. Once you find the right kind they will keep, stored away from the light, for up to one year. The Food Glossary (p. 216) has descriptions of the different varieties used in this book.

Finally, a confession. Despite a larder very full of these wondrous nuggets, I often find myself using cans of chickpeas or kidney beans. I am not much of a fan of canned lentils but canned beans do make life a lot easier and they work wonderfully in Indian dishes.

sunny lentil curry
PEELI DAL

This small yellow lentil is the split and skinned green mung bean. It is the lightest and easiest to digest of all the lentils and has a subtle buttery flavour. This mild dish is a staple in most north Indian households and is cooked practically every other day. If you do not like mountains of spice in your Indian food, give this a try. Asafoetida is an extremely pungent spice but it does impart a subtle background flavour and importantly helps in making lentils easier to digest.

Serves 4-6

200g (7 oz) skinned and split (yellow) mung lentils (*dhuli hui moong dal*), picked over and washed
1 litre (1½ pints) cold water
1–2 green chillies, halved lengthways
½ tsp turmeric powder
4cm (1½ inch) piece of fresh ginger, peeled and cut into fine shreds

salt to taste
2 medium tomatoes, ground
1½ tsp vegetable oil
1 level tsp cumin seeds
1 pinch of asafoetida (optional)
½ tsp garam masala
a handful of chopped fresh coriander (leaves and stalks)

Place the lentils, water, chilli, turmeric, ginger and salt in a saucepan, bring to the boil and boil for 2–3 minutes. Turn the heat down, partially cover and simmer for about 15 minutes. Skim off any scum that forms on the surface with a metal spoon. If the curry starts to rise, lower the heat until it settles. If you can't give the pan your full attention, cook uncovered on a low heat, adding an extra 200ml (7 fl oz) water and an extra 10 minutes cooking time.

Add the tomatoes and cook until the lentils start to break down and cloud the water, a further 20 minutes or so. Add more water from the kettle for a thinner consistency, remembering that this curry thickens as it cools.

Heat the oil in a small non-stick frying pan. Add the cumin and asafoetida (if using) and fry until fragrant, about 30 seconds. Pour in some of the curry, stir to mix and then pour back into the saucepan together with the garam masala and coriander. Serve hot.

This full-bodied curry is typical North Indian peasant fare. It is earthy, nutritious and goes with any meat or vegetable. The lentils do not need to be soaked but do take a while to cook. A pressure cooker will cut down the cooking time to 30–40 minutes and give excellent results. Serve this hearty dish with *roti* (p. 34) a 'dry' lamb or chicken dish and potatoes for a warm winter's meal, or eat with a hunk of bread as a warming winter soup.

punjabi peasant lentil curry
MACHOLLE KI DAL

LENTILS

100g (3½ oz) split black gram (*ma ki dal*), picked over and washed thoroughly

50g (1¾ oz) split Bengal gram (*channa dal*), picked over and washed thoroughly

2 small tomatoes, ground

3 garlic cloves, grated

5cm (2 inch) piece of fresh ginger, peeled and cut into fine shreds

1–2 green chillies, halved lengthways

800ml (28 fl oz) cold water

salt to taste

TARKA

2 tsp butter

1 tsp vegetable oil

1 small onion, chopped

1 tsp cumin seeds

½ tsp garlic, finely chopped

½ tsp red chilli powder

½ tsp garam masala

a handful of chopped fresh coriander (leaves and stalks)

Serves 4–5

Place all the ingredients for the lentils in a heavy-based saucepan. Bring to the boil, cover and simmer over a low heat, until the lentils are plump and have started to break down to merge with the water, about 60–70 minutes. Stir every so often and make sure there is enough water in the pan. Season.

Meanwhile, make the *tarka*. Heat the butter and oil in a non-stick frying pan and gently brown the onion, 8–10 minutes. Add the cumin and fry until fragrant, about 30 seconds. Add the garlic and chilli powder, and cook for 1 further minute. Pour a little of the curry into the pan, mix well and pour back into the curry. Stir in the garam masala and coriander and serve hot.

Punjabi Peasant Lentil Curry with Fenugreek Leavened Bread

earthy green lentil curry
MOONG KI DAL

This rustic curry, made from split mung beans, also known as 'broken' mung beans, has a savoury and earthy flavour. You can buy split beans in Indian stores or you can give the whole beans one or two pulses in a food processor. A quick whirl with the hand blender will turn the finished dish into delicious, wholesome soup to eat with a chunk of fresh bread.

Serves 3–4 (quantities can be doubled)

100g (3½ oz) split mung lentils (*moong dal*), picked over and washed
4cm (1½ inch) piece of fresh ginger, peeled and cut into fine shreds
1–2 green chillies, left whole
½ tsp turmeric powder
700ml (1½ pints) cold water
1 tsp salt
2 small tomatoes, grated
1 tsp vegetable oil
½ tsp cumin seeds
½ tsp garam masala
a handful of chopped fresh coriander (leaves and stalks)

Place the lentils, ginger, chillies, turmeric, water and salt in a large saucepan and bring to the boil. Continue to boil for about 10 minutes, then turn the heat down to low, cover and simmer for about 25 minutes, stirring occasionally.

Add the tomatoes, cover again and cook for a further 15–20 minutes or until the lentils are tender, have amalgamated with the water and the whole curry comes together. Stir occasionally and add more water if necessary.

Heat the oil in a small non-stick frying pan and fry the cumin seeds until fragrant, about 30–40 seconds. Add a couple of spoonfuls of the lentils, mix well and then stir the whole mixture back into the lentils. Adjust the seasoning, stir in the garam masala and coriander and serve hot.

This is my favourite everyday lentil dish. The goodness and flavour of five kinds of lentil are packed into this super-healthy, super-easy and, of course, super-tasty dish. Each lentil adds its own flavour and texture so that every mouthful promises myriad flavours. If you can't get hold of all of them, just add more of the others. I always leave the chillies whole in this recipe as the flavour really adds something but without imparting too much heat. You can always chop it up for that not-so-subtle bite.

mixed lentil curry
PANCHRANGI DAL

Serves 4

2 medium tomatoes, grated
2 tsp vegetable oil
2 tbs onion, chopped
1 tsp cumin seeds
½ tsp garlic, chopped
½ tsp garam masala
a handful of chopped fresh coriander (leaves and stalks)

CURRY
1½ tbs each of split and skinned mung beans (*dhuli hui moong dal*), split black gram (*ma ki dal*), split pigeon peas (*toovar dal*) and Bengal gram (*channa dal*), picked over and washed thoroughly
3 tbs red lentils (*masoor dal*)
750ml (25 fl oz) cold water
1 heaped tsp fresh ginger, chopped
2 tsp garlic, chopped
½ tsp turmeric powder
2 green chillies, left whole
1 good tsp salt

Place all the curry ingredients in a heavy-bottomed saucepan. Bring to the boil and then cook, covered, on the lowest heat for 25 minutes. Keep skimming any scum off the top with a metal spoon.

Add the tomatoes and continue cooking until the lentils have started to break down, another 10 minutes. The water and lentils will have merged together into one beautiful creamy mass yet retaining lots of texture.

Meanwhile, heat the oil in a small non-stick frying pan. Fry the onion until golden, about 5–6 minutes, lowering the heat once it starts to colour. Add the cumin and garlic, and cook for 1 further minute over a low heat.

Pour some of the lentils into this pan, mix well and pour into the curry. Stir in the garam masala and coriander and serve hot.

hot split pigeon pea curry
LASAN WALI TOOVAR KI DAL

A dish so simple that anyone can make it. The lentils themselves are savoury and earthy, and the garlic and chillies give the dish all the flavour it needs. Don't be afraid of the amount of chillies; leaving them whole adds flavour without heat. It really doesn't get any easier; a stunning store-cupboard dish. Mustard oil does add an extra flavour but you can use a simple vegetable oil.

Serves 2-3 (quantities can be doubled)

650ml (22 fl oz) cold water
100g (3½ oz) split pigeon peas (*toovar dal*), picked over and washed
½ tsp turmeric powder
salt to taste

2 tsp mustard or vegetable oil
1 rounded tbs garlic, chopped
3–4 small dried red chillies, left whole, or crushed red chillies to taste
1 level tsp dried mango powder

Place the water and lentils in a saucepan and bring to the boil. Add the turmeric and salt, cover and simmer over a low heat until tender, about 45–55 minutes. The lentils should just start to break down. Adjust the seasoning. Reduce the gravy over a high heat if it is too watery or add more water from the kettle if necessary. It should have the texture of thick but not mushy soup. Take off the heat.

Heat the oil in a small non-stick saucepan. Add the garlic and sauté for 10 seconds, then add the chillies. Cook until the garlic is golden, then pour a few spoonfuls of the lentils into the pan, mix well and stir back into the curry along with the dried mango powder. Serve hot.

Hot Split Pigeon Pea Curry with Tangy Tomato Rice

vegetable and lentil curry
SAAMBAR

This thin, spicy and tangy curry is a southern staple. You can buy *saambar* powder and canned drumsticks in Indian shops. Serve with *Rice and Lentil Pancakes* (p. 164), *Quick Coconut Chutney* (p. 185) and/or *Tangy Tomato Chutney* (p. 186).

1 tbs + 1 tsp vegetable oil
1 small onion, sliced
1 tsp garlic paste
1 tsp brown mustard seeds
15 fresh or dried curry leaves
½ tsp black peppercorns
2–3 small dried red chillies
1 rounded tsp coriander powder
salt to taste
1 tbs *saambar* powder or to taste
1 medium tomato, cut into wedges
1–2 tsp tamarind paste *or* 30g (1 oz) block of tamarind, soaked and juice extracted (see p. 27) or to taste

CURRY
100g (3½ oz) split pigeon peas (*toovar dal*), picked over and washed
½ tsp turmeric powder
800ml (28 fl oz) cold water
½ each aubergine and bottle gourd, cut into 5cm (2 inch) cubes
2 small potatoes, cut into 4cm (1½ inch) cubes
200g (7 oz) fresh or canned drumsticks, cut into 8cm (3¼ inch) pieces and washed thoroughly

Serves 3–4

Place the lentils, turmeric and water in a large saucepan. Bring to the boil, cover and cook on a low to moderate heat for 40–45 minutes, adding the vegetables half way. Stir occasionally. Once the lentils and vegetables are tender, mash some of both with the back of a spoon to thicken the curry.

Meanwhile, heat 1 tablespoon of the oil in a large non-stick frying pan and fry the onion until just golden, about 8 minutes. Add the garlic and cook for 30 seconds. Push the onion to one side of the pan, pour the teaspoon of oil into the centre and add the mustard seeds, curry leaves, peppercorns, chillies (if using), coriander powder, salt and *saambar* powder to the oil. Cook for 15 seconds then combine with the onion. Cook for 1 further minute and stir into the cooked curry, together with the tomato. Cook for 10 minutes, adding the tamarind halfway through. The curry should have the consistency of thin soup.

This popular street fare is spicy and tangy and very, very moreish. It is normally paired with fried leavened bread (*bhatura*). At home I prefer healthier food, so I serve it with *Charred (Nearly) Flat-Bread*, (p. 109) for a more digestible meal. It will soon become a household favourite. Dried and soaked chickpeas are ideal (when cooking, add a teabag, 2 bay leaves, 3 cloves, 3 black cardamom pods, 1 whole cinnamon stick and a good pinch of bicarbonate of soda). Happily, however, canned chickpeas also give excellent results. If you are nervous about the spices, add a little at a time and keep tasting.

tangy spicy chickpeas
CHATTPATTE CHOLLE

Serves 4 (quantities can be halved)

1½ tbs vegetable oil
1 medium onion, chopped
4cm (1½ inch) piece of fresh ginger, peeled and cut into fine shreds
1 medium tomato, chopped
1–2 green chillies, left whole, or halved lengthways
2 tsp coriander powder
salt to taste
125ml (4½ fl oz) hot water or cooking liquid
500g (1 lb 2 oz) can of chickpeas *or*

200g (7 oz) dried chickpeas (*kabuli channa/cholle*), soaked overnight and cooked as directed on p. 22 in 1.5 litres (48 fl oz) water, reserving the cooking liquor
2 rounded tsp each of dried pomegranate seeds and roasted cumin powder
1 tsp *channa masala*
½ tsp garam masala
chopped fresh coriander and thin raw onion and tomato slices to garnish

Heat the oil in a non-stick saucepan. Add the onion and fry for 3 minutes, then add the ginger and continue cooking over a low heat until golden, about 12–14 minutes.

Follow with the tomato, chilli, coriander powder and salt. Cook, stirring, over a moderate heat for 6–8 minutes, adding 2 tablespoons of the water or cooking liquor if the pan becomes dry.

Add the chickpeas and the remaining water or cooking liquid, bring to the boil and simmer for 5 minutes. Add the remaining spices and cook until most of the liquid has evaporated. Serve hot, garnished with the fresh coriander, onion and tomato slices.

IF WE HAD a penny for every time we've been advised to eat our vegetables, the only thing that would be fat would be our wallets! You can hardly read a magazine or watch the news without being reminded to eat between five and seven portions of fruit and vegetables a day.

They're right, of course (*they* always are!). Vegetables are nature's way of taking care of us. I find it hard to stop myself from extolling the health properties of each individual vegetable as I'm so amazed by how beneficial they can be. This food group is packed with vitamins, minerals and antioxidants. Vegetables are a great source of soluble fibre and, being mostly water, they are both filling and hydrating: great for those with small appetites. All in all, vegetables help keep our bodies at their optimum levels.

VERSATILE **VEGETABLES**

In India, a meal without a vegetable is incomplete. If the worst came to the worst, we would add vegetables to one of the other rice, lentil, or meat dishes. I can't ever remember uneaten veggies being an issue when I was growing up, as they were such a normal part of our diet. In fact, most curries are made up of onions, tomatoes, ginger and garlic, so you are getting a wealth of goodness in every bite.

Luckily, I have become an unabashed vegetable lover and really appreciate their inherent flavours. I do attribute this to Indian food as the added flavours make simple vegetables truly appetising. Serve these dishes as part of an Indian meal or jazz up your normal fare by adding a little spice to your 'meat and two veg'.

This is a classic Punjabi dish where buttery potatoes are paired with flavourful cauliflower. It is simple to make and absolutely addictive. The asafoetida makes the cauliflower easier to digest but it's not essential. The dried mango powder lifts all the flavours of the dish, but as a substitute throw a tomato in with the other vegetables and sharpen with lemon juice. Don't worry about making too much, the leftovers make great samosas (p. 106), grilled sandwiches and stuffed breads (see Leftovers?).

potatoes with cauliflower
ALOO GHOBI

1 tbs vegetable oil
1 tsp cumin seeds
1 pinch of asafoetida (optional)
1–2 green chillies, seeded and sliced
   (optional)
5cm (2 inch) piece of fresh ginger,
   peeled and cut into fine shreds
½ tsp turmeric powder
1½ tsp coriander powder
salt to taste

1 small head of cauliflower, cut into
   large florets
300g (10½ oz) new potatoes, peeled
   and cut into thick wedges
½ tsp each dried mango powder and
   garam masala
2 tsp dried fenugreek leaves,
   crumbled
a small handful of chopped fresh
   coriander (leaves and stalks)
   to garnish

Serves 4-6

Heat the oil in a non-stick saucepan and fry the cumin seeds and asafoetida (if using) for about 30 seconds. Turn the heat down; add the chillies (if using) and the ginger, and stir-fry for 30 seconds before adding the turmeric, coriander powder and salt.

Add the vegetables and stir to coat well in the spices. Add a good splash of hot water, cover and cook over a low heat until the vegetables are tender, about 15–20 minutes. Stir occasionally and add a splash of hot water if the pan gets dry.

Uncover the pan and dry off any excess water over a high heat while gently tossing the vegetables. Stir in the mango powder, garam masala and fenugreek leaves. Serve hot, garnished with the fresh coriander.

peppery hot cabbage salad
BAND GHOBI KA SALADE

This is so simple to make, yet it is one of the tastiest cabbage dishes; it puts sauerkraut to shame. The flavours are clean and powerful, peppery rather than spicy. In fact, you can leave out the chillies altogether, although they do add an extra dimension as does the mustard oil. This dish can be eaten as a hot salad or as a meal accompaniment. It goes really well with other south Indian flavours; try it with *Semolina Pilaff* (p. 47).

Serves 2–3 (quantities can be doubled)

2 tsp mustard or vegetable oil
1 scant pinch of asafoetida
1 tsp each brown mustard and nigella
 (onion) seeds
10–15 fresh or dried curry leaves
2 small dried red chillies, left whole
 (optional)

1 tsp skinned and split black gram
 (*urad dal*), picked over and washed
1 tbs peanuts, chopped
½ large head of cabbage, finely
 shredded
salt to taste

Heat the oil in a large non-stick saucepan. Add the asafoetida and seeds, and fry for 30 seconds. Then add the curry leaves, chillies (if using), lentils and peanuts. Turn the heat down and fry for 30 seconds. Add the cabbage and salt, and stir-fry for 10 minutes. The cabbage should be wilted, yet retain some bite.

Peppery Hot Cabbage Salad shown with Uppma

These meaty yet melting mushrooms are lifted out of the ordinary in a spicy, smooth sauce. This is my favourite mushroom dish. To give it an elegant twist on a special occasion, I use a mixture of exotic or wild mushrooms. Use leftovers to stuff a *parantha* (p. 176) or samosa (p. 106), or pile up on a couple of wedges of toast for a light lunch.

melt-in-your-mouth mushrooms
MASALA KHUMBI

1½ tbs vegetable oil

1 large onion, finely chopped

2 tsp garlic paste

1 tsp ginger paste

½ tsp each of turmeric and red chilli powders

2 tsp coriander powder

1 rounded tsp garam masala

salt to taste

2 medium tomatoes, chopped

Serves 4

100ml (3½ fl oz) hot water

15g (½ oz) raw cashew nuts, soaked in boiling water for 30 minutes, drained and pounded to a paste

450g (1 lb) button or chestnut mushrooms, wiped with a damp cloth and thickly sliced

2 tsp cumin powder

a handful of chopped fresh coriander (leaves and stalks)

Heat the oil in a non-stick saucepan and fry the onion. Turn the heat down once the onion starts to colour and stir often until golden brown and shrivelled up, about 10 minutes. Add water to the pan to prevent burning, if necessary.

Add the garlic and ginger pastes, and cook for 1 minute, adding the turmeric, chilli, coriander powder, garam masala and salt halfway through cooking. Stir in the tomatoes and water and cook over a moderate heat for 15 minutes, adding splashes of water from the kettle when necessary. Stir in the nut paste.

Add the mushrooms, cover and cook over a moderate heat until done, stirring often, about 10 minutes. Uncover and turn up the heat to dry off any excess liquid. Stir in the cumin and fresh coriander and serve hot.

'creamy' bottle gourd
DAHI WALA GHIYA

This dish is too homely to be found on restaurant menus, but that is their loss, as it is a great recipe. It is only lightly spiced so as to not overpower the gourd's own subtle character. *Dudhi* is normally cooked with tomatoes but the yoghurt adds creaminess as well as a tang. You will be amazed that such simple ingredients can create such a flavourful dish.

1½ tsp vegetable oil
1 tbs garlic, finely chopped
1 heaped tsp fresh ginger, finely
   chopped
½ tsp each turmeric and red chilli
   powders
1 tsp coriander powder
salt to taste

2 medium bottle gourds (*dudhis*),
   peeled and cut into 2.5cm (1 inch)
   cubes
2 tbs low-fat yoghurt, beaten
½ tsp cumin powder
½ tsp each garam masala, black
   pepper and dried mango powder
a small handful of chopped fresh
   coriander (leaves and stalks)

Serves 3–4

Heat the oil in a non-stick saucepan and fry the garlic and ginger until lightly coloured, about 30–40 seconds. Add the turmeric, chilli, coriander powder and salt, stir for 10 seconds, then add the vegetable. Toss well to mix and add a good splash of water from the kettle.

Bring to the boil, then simmer, covered, until the vegetable is cooked, between 20 and 45 minutes, depending on its freshness. Stir occasionally and make sure there is enough liquid; if not add a splash from the kettle.

Once the vegetable is tender, uncover and dry off any excess liquid over a high heat. Stir in the yoghurt a tablespoonful at a time and cook for 3–4 minutes. The whole dish should then amalgamate and the pieces of vegetable will stick together. Add the remaining spices and fresh coriander, and serve hot.

spinach and mung bean purée
SAAG

The sharpness often found in spinach is mellowed by the mung beans in this delicious vegetable purée. This basic dish lends itself to a lot of variations. One of my favourites is to add a handful of fresh dill towards the end, as in this recipe. However, it can be omitted completely. Another classic variation is to replace half of the spinach with fresh mustard leaves. Delicious served with flat-bread and lamb.

SPINACH PURÉE

500g (1 lb 2 oz) fresh spinach, picked over, tough stalks removed and washed in at least three changes of water

50g (1¾ oz) whole green mung beans (*sabut moong*), picked over and washed

1–2 green chillies, left whole

1 tsp fresh ginger, chopped

2 fat garlic cloves, roughly chopped

250ml (9 fl oz) cold water

1 tsp salt or to taste

TARKA

2 tsp vegetable oil

1 small onion, chopped

2 garlic cloves, finely chopped

1 tsp coriander seeds, roughly crushed, or coriander powder

up to 200ml (7 fl oz) hot water

3 generous tbs low-fat yoghurt, beaten

1 large handful of chopped fresh dill (optional)

1 tsp butter

1–2 tsp lemon juice or to taste

Serves 4

Place all the ingredients for the spinach purée in a heavy-based saucepan. Simmer, covered, until the beans are tender, about 40–45 minutes. Process or blend into a smooth purée. Return to a low heat.

Next, make the *tarka*. Heat the oil in a non-stick frying pan and sauté the onion until golden, about 8–10 minutes. Stir in the garlic and the coriander, and cook for about 30–40 seconds. Stir into the spinach, together with enough water for a smooth but not thick purée, the yoghurt, a tablespoonful at a time, and the dill (if using). Cook for 1 further minute. Taste, adjust the seasoning and stir in the butter and lemon juice to taste. Heat through for 2–3 minutes and serve hot.

It is hard to describe the intensity of flavours in this dish but I can definitely say that no one can ever again proclaim that vegetables are boring. Each bite reveals a stratum of exciting tastes. It is also incredibly easy to cook. I use small Japanese-style aubergines that are easily available in India, but the size is not important. You can use larger ones chopped into 2.5cm (1 inch) pieces. Small waxy potatoes are best as they retain their shape and the mustard oil is authentic and preferable for this dish.

aubergine and potatoes with pickling spices

AACHAARI ALOO BAINGAN

1 tbs mustard or vegetable oil	450g (1 lb) baby aubergines
½ tsp each cumin, nigella (onion) and	(around 10), washed and quartered
fenugreek seeds	lengthways
1 tsp each brown mustard and	225g (8 oz) waxy new potatoes, peeled
fennel seeds	and cut into wedges
5cm (2 inch) piece of fresh ginger,	2 medium tomatoes, sliced into
peeled and cut into fine shreds	wedges
1 tsp garlic, chopped	100ml (3½ fl oz) hot water
1 rounded tsp coriander powder	½ level tsp garam masala
½ tsp turmeric powder	lemon juice to taste
¼–½ tsp red chilli powder or to taste	a handful of chopped fresh coriander
salt to taste	(leaves and stalks)

Serves 4

Heat the oil in a non-stick saucepan and fry the seeds for about 30–40 seconds. Add the ginger, garlic, coriander powder, turmeric, chilli and salt, and cook for 20 seconds.

Add the aubergines and potatoes and a splash of hot water. Stir for 2–3 minutes, then cover and cook over a low heat for 10 minutes. Add the tomatoes and the water, and cook over a moderate heat for 10 minutes, when the vegetables should be tender. Uncover and reduce the excess liquid over a high heat or add extra water from the kettle as necessary.

Stir in the garam masala, lemon juice and fresh coriander, and serve hot.

spiced colocasia
MASALE WALI ARBI

If you have never tried this vegetable, you are missing out.

This sturdy root vegetable has a dark brown skin and is similar to the potato except that the flesh is creamier. Colocasia is hard to come by but is worth seeking out at your closest ethnic market.

This recipe is a great complement to your usual roast dishes, as part of your Indian meal or simply eaten with freshly made *Layered Flat-Bread* (p. 134).

Serves 4–6

550g (1 lb 4 oz) colocasia, washed
2 tbs vegetable oil
1½ tsp carom seeds
¼–½ tsp red chilli powder
½ tsp dried mango powder
1 tbs coriander powder
1 tsp salt or to taste
3 tbs chopped fresh coriander
 (leaves and stalks)

Boil the colocasia in plenty of salted water until fork-tender, about 20–30 minutes. Once cool enough to handle, scrape off the skin and quarter into wedges. Set aside.

Heat the oil in a non-stick saucepan and fry the carom seeds for 10 seconds. Turn the heat down and stir in the chilli, mango and coriander powders, and the salt.

Add the colocasia, increase the heat, and carefully stir-fry over a high heat for 5 minutes. The wedges should develop a slight crust and be coated in the spices.

Adjust the seasoning if necessary and serve hot, garnished with the fresh coriander.

Spiced Colocasia on Layered Flat-Bread

veggie dumpling curry
GHIYA KA KOFTA CURRY

These dumplings are very popular in certain regions of north India and are traditionally made with either cabbage, lotus root or bottle gourd and then deep-fried. I add a little extra gram flour to help bind them then boil them and, when cooked, pop them straight into the gravy so that they absorb its flavours.

Serves 2-3 (quantities can be doubled)

1 tbs vegetable oil
½ tsp each garlic and ginger pastes
1 medium tomato, grated
salt to taste
2 heaped tbs *Everyday Curry Paste* (p. 28)
½ tsp red chilli powder
50ml (2 fl oz) milk
2 tsp low-fat yoghurt, beaten
1 scant tbs dried fenugreek leaves, crumbled
a small handful of chopped fresh coriander (leaves and stalks)

DUMPLINGS
400g (14 oz) bottle gourd (*dudhi*), peeled and coarsely grated
4 heaped tbs gram flour (*besan*)
½ tsp each red chilli powder and garam masala
½ tsp each salt and dried pomegranate powder
1 tbs chopped fresh coriander

First, make the dumplings. Boil the bottle gourd for 5–7 minutes, until firm to the touch. Drain and reserve the cooking liquid, then squeeze out most of the excess from the vegetable and discard. Add the remaining dumpling ingredients and combine but do not overwork.

With clean but moist hands, make little balls from the mixture; you should get about 8. Boil in salted water for 8–10 minutes. Drain and set aside, reserving the cooking liquid.

Heat the oil in a small non-stick saucepan. Add the ginger and garlic pastes, followed by the tomato and salt. Cook for 1–2 minutes over a moderate heat, reducing until pulpy. Add the curry paste, chilli, milk and yoghurt and stir to mix. Add 300ml (10 fl oz) water from the reserved cooking liquids. Bring to the boil and simmer gently for 4–5 minutes. Stir in the yoghurt and fenugreek leaves.

Add the cooked dumplings and gently spoon the sauce over them. Cook for another 5 minutes until the sauce is thick. Stir in the fresh coriander and serve hot.

The flavours of this dish overwhelm the taste buds as they unfold to reveal a wealth of layers. This thick mash has a creamy, smoky character that you would never associate with a healthy vegetarian dish. I always make extra as it makes a great leftover ingredient that works with many different meals. Use to fill a toasted cheese sandwich, stir a spoonful into a little yoghurt and serve as a dip, or stuff in a pitta bread along with salad and a chunky *raita* for a perfect, light lunch.

smoky aubergine mash
BAIGAN KA BHARTA

Serves 4–6

3 medium aubergines
1½ tbs vegetable oil
1 medium onion, finely chopped
2.5cm (1 inch) piece of fresh ginger, peeled and cut into fine strips
1–2 green chillies, seeded and chopped (optional)
1 tsp coriander powder

salt to taste
2 medium tomatoes, chopped
1 rounded tsp tomato purée
100g (3½ oz) shelled green peas, fresh or frozen (optional)
½ tsp garam masala
a handful of chopped fresh coriander (leaves and stalks)

Preheat the oven to 200°C/400°F/Gas 6. Prick the aubergines all over and grill or roast in the preheated oven until the skins are charred and blistered all over, around 20 minutes, turning often. When cool enough to handle, peel off the skins and roughly mash the flesh.

Meanwhile, heat the oil in a non-stick saucepan and sauté the onion until golden, about 8–10 minutes. Add the ginger and chilli (if using), and cook for 40 seconds. Stir in the coriander powder and salt. Stir for 1 minute, then add the tomatoes, tomato purée and peas (if using). Cook for about 4 minutes until the tomatoes are pulpy.

Add the aubergine flesh and cook, stirring, until all the excess water released by the vegetable has dried off, around 10 minutes.

Stir in the garam masala and the fresh coriander, and serve hot or at room temperature.

I SEEM TO be bumping into more and more people who have to limit or completely omit wheat from their diet. Many suffer from wheat or gluten allergies while others are simply trying to vary what they eat and wean themselves off their wheat dependence. I once gave up wheat for three months to see if it had any effect on my health and shape. It didn't, but I did start to appreciate and enjoy other sources of carbohydrates. We are encouraged to eat a varied diet to get a broad range of nutrients and this is a good way to start.

WHEAT-FREE AND **HAPPY**

Many north Indians consider a meal without bread to be something akin to a gallery with state-of-the-art security, seating and ambient music, but no art. But we do eat flat-breads made from grains other than wheat, depending on the season and what they are being served with. However, most Indians eat quantities of rice, which is consumed in some form at practically every meal. In fact, rice is such an important part of our culinary make-up that it is used in both sweet and savoury dishes, where it can be roasted, flaked, beaten, ground, fried, boiled and puffed.

Rice can be dressed up to be the star of the meal or served plain to absorb the other flavours. It is one of the most versatile grains and is underrated by many Western cuisines. In the north, we use delicate and fragrant long-grained rice, whereas southerners cultivate a thicker, coarser grain. Essentially, you can use either but most of these recipes would be better enjoyed with the long-grained variety. See p. 33 for tips on cooking rice, but do remember to wash the grains in several changes of clean water and soak them for 30 minutes before cooking. Remember that if you do not soak the rice the proportion of water to rice increases to 1 part rice to 2 parts water.

I have included a wheat-free bread and a few regional speciality dishes. Where relevant, I have explained how these dishes are traditionally eaten and what the appropriate accompaniments would be. Potatoes are another excellent non-wheat source of carbohydrate; look in the index for specific recipes.

simple, spiced saffron rice
KESARI PULLAO

This stunning but simple rice dish is inspired by the Persian pilaffs that have become popular in the north of India. It is delicately spiced with whole spices and has a sprinkling of sultanas and almonds for sweetness and texture, which is characteristic of Persian-influenced cooking. Wonderful served with chicken and lamb dishes.

1 tbs vegetable oil
1 small onion, finely sliced
½ tsp saffron strands
2 tbs golden sultanas
10 almonds, blanched, peeled and halved lengthways
200g (7 oz) Basmati or long-grained rice, washed, and soaked for 30 minutes
375ml (12 fl oz) hot water

salt to taste
1–2 tsp lemon juice or to taste

WHOLE SPICES
1 rounded tsp cumin seeds
2 each brown cardamom pods, green cardamom pods and bay leaves, lightly crushed
5cm (2 inch) cinnamon stick, halved

Serves 4

Heat the oil in a heavy-based non-stick saucepan. Add the onion and sauté until lightly caramelised, about 8 minutes. Add the whole spices, saffron, sultanas and almonds and stir-fry until fragrant, about 30–40 seconds.

Add the drained rice, water and salt. Stir and taste the water for salt and adjust if necessary. Bring to the boil, cover and cook, undisturbed, on the lowest heat possible for 10–12 minutes.

The grains should be just tender. Take off the heat and leave to steam, covered and undisturbed, for a further 10 minutes. Uncover, stir in the lemon juice, fluffing up the rice with a fork, and serve hot.

vegetable biryani
SABZI KI BIRYANI

Traditionally, a biryani is an elaborate rice dish, made with meat, yoghurt, saffron, nuts and stomach-churning amounts of butter. However, I make this vegetarian version quite often. It is simplified so that you can cook it in one pan, and it is healthy enough to be everyday fare. Despite the long list of ingredients, this is a really quick and easy recipe. Use your favourite vegetables and leave out anything that doesn't appeal.

Serves 3
(quantities
can be
doubled)

1 tbs vegetable oil
1 small onion, sliced
½ tsp each of ginger and garlic pastes
½ tsp turmeric powder
1 good pinch of red chilli powder
1 tsp coriander powder
salt to taste
1 small carrot, 1 small potato and
   1 medium tomato, chopped
50g (1¾ oz) cauliflower florets
4 tbs low-fat yoghurt, beaten
1 tbs ground almonds
a small handful of shelled green peas,
   fresh or frozen, or canned
   chickpeas
190ml (6½ fl oz) hot water

100g (3½ oz) Basmati or long-grained
   rice, washed, and soaked for
   30 minutes
1 good pinch of saffron strands,
   infused in 2 tbs hot milk
lemon juice to taste
a handful of chopped fresh coriander
   (leaves and stalks)

WHOLE SPICES
1 each brown cardamom pod, green
   cardamom pod and large bay leaf
2 cloves
1 whole cinnamon stick, 5–7.5cm
   (2–3 inches)
1 tsp cumin seeds

Heat the oil in a non-stick saucepan. Fry the onion until soft and just coloured, about 6–7 minutes. Add the whole spices, ginger and garlic pastes, and stir-fry for about 30–40 seconds.

Add the turmeric, chilli and coriander powders, the salt and the prepared vegetables; sauté for 2–3 minutes. Cover and cook for 10 minutes on a low heat, stirring often, adding a splash of water if necessary. Stir in the yoghurt, a tablespoonful at a time, and the ground almonds. Reduce any excess liquid over a moderate heat. Add the peas or chickpeas and the water. Taste and adjust the seasoning.

Stir in the drained rice. Bring to the boil, cover, then turn the heat as low as possible and cook, undisturbed, for about 12 minutes. Check after 10 minutes. When the grains are just tender, take off the heat and leave to steam, covered and undisturbed, for a further 10 minutes.

Drizzle over the saffron, and if the yoghurt has not made the dish sufficiently tart, add the lemon juice. Fluff up with a fork, sprinkle over the fresh coriander and serve hot.

quick vegetable pilaff
SABZI KI PULLAO

A quick rice pilaff with whole spices that uses leftover cooked rice and vegetables.

2 tsp vegetable oil
½ small onion, sliced
2.5cm (1 inch) cinnamon stick
1 each of green cardamom pod, black cardamom pod and bay leaf
½ tsp cumin seeds
2 cloves

3 black peppercorns
200g (7 oz) leftover cooked vegetables (such as cauliflower florets, peas and carrots)
salt to taste
400ml (13 fl oz) leftover cooked rice
squeeze of lemon juice

Serves 2

Heat the oil in a large non-stick saucepan. Add the onion and sauté until soft and lightly golden, about 4–5 minutes. Add the spices and cook until fragrant, about 30 seconds.

Add the vegetables and salt, and cook gently for 3–4 minutes to heat through. Taste and adjust the seasoning, if necessary.

Add the rice and gently stir-fry for 1–2 minutes to heat through. Stir in the lemon juice with a fork to fluff up the rice and serve.

An unusual rice dish of interesting flavours and a delicate colour. Not a typical north Indian dish but it can be found in the house of one adventurous cook. I find the delicate sweetness of the fennel seeds contrasts superbly with the tart tomatoes and the spicy chillies. Serve with chicken, fish or prawns for a symphony of harmonious taste notes.

tangy tomato rice
TAMATAR KA PULLAO

Serves 4

1 tbs vegetable oil
1 tsp cumin seeds
1 medium onion, sliced
2 medium tomatoes, ground
2 tsp tomato purée
1 good pinch of chilli powder
salt to taste
375ml (12 fl oz) hot water

200g (7 oz) Basmati or long-grained
   rice, washed, and soaked for
   30 minutes
1 heaped tsp fennel seeds, roughly
   pounded in a pestle and mortar
lemon juice to taste
a handful of chopped fresh coriander
   (leaves and stalks)

Heat the oil in a heavy non-stick saucepan. Add the cumin seeds and fry for 30 seconds. Add the onion and sauté until soft and golden, turning the heat down once it starts to colour, about 8 minutes.

Add the tomatoes, tomato purée, chilli and salt. Reduce for 8–10 minutes until thick.

Stir in the water, drained rice and fennel seeds and stir again. Taste the water for salt and adjust if necessary. Bring to the boil, then turn down the heat as low as possible, cover tightly and simmer, undisturbed, for 10–12 minutes. Check after 10 minutes. Once the rice is done, turn off the heat and leave to steam, covered and undisturbed, for 10 minutes.

Taste and, if necessary, drizzle with lemon juice. Fluff up with a fork and garnish with the coriander. Serve hot.

carrot pilaff
GAJAR KA PULLAO

This dish is spectacular in many ways. The vibrant orange carrots add colour, sweetness and texture to the fragrant rice. The ratio of vegetable to rice is higher than you would normally find in a vegetable pilaff but it is a very pleasing combination and the carrot is nutritious, as well as adding bulk. It is so delicious that I serve it to guests as often as I make it for myself, either as part of a meal or on its own.

Serves 2-3
(quantities
can be
doubled)

2 tsp vegetable oil
½ small onion, sliced
2.5cm (1 inch) cinnamon stick
1 each green cardamom pod, brown cardamom pod and bay leaf, lightly crushed
½ tsp cumin seeds
1 medium-sized carrot, peeled and coarsely grated

½ tsp salt or to taste
100g (3½ oz) Basmati or long-grained rice, washed, and soaked for 30 minutes
190ml (6½ fl oz) hot water
1 tsp lemon juice or to taste
a handful of chopped fresh coriander to garnish

Heat the oil in a small non-stick saucepan and sauté the onion until golden, around 6–8 minutes, lowering the heat once it starts to colour. Add the spices and cook until fragrant, about 20 seconds. Add the carrot and salt and sauté for 1 minute.

Stir in the drained rice and water; taste the water for salt and adjust if necessary. Bring to the boil, then cover and cook, undisturbed, on the lowest heat possible for 10–12 minutes. Check that the rice is just tender, then take off the heat and leave to steam, covered and undisturbed, for another 10 minutes.

Stir in the lemon juice with a fork and fluff up the grains. Garnish with the coriander and serve hot.

rice and lentil pancakes
DOSA

A *dosa* is a large, thin, crisp pancake made with a rice and lentil batter. It is like bread to the southern Indians and is eaten practically every day. It can be served as it is, or filled with a variety of ingredients, normally *Potatoes with Onions and Mustard Seeds* (p. 131) and served with *Quick Coconut Chutney* (p. 185) or with *Tangy Tomato Chutney* (p. 186) and with a thin *Vegetable and Lentil Curry* (p. 144). You do have to soak the grains overnight. (If skinned black gram are not available, after soaking overnight, rub the lentils in a tea towel to remove the skins.) Make these pancakes in the biggest non-stick frying pan you have. A food processor is essential for this recipe.

Makes 4–5

100g (3½ oz) Basmati or long-grained rice, washed and drained
50g (1¾ oz) skinned and split black gram (*urad dal*), picked over and washed

180–200ml (6–7 fl oz) cold water
1 good pinch of salt
2 tbs vegetable oil

Soak the rice and lentils overnight.

The following day drain and discard the soaking liquid. Grind to a fine paste using a food processor. Add enough water to make a smooth batter with the consistency of double cream. Add the salt.

Allow the batter to ferment for 4–5 hours in a warm place until frothy, such as inside an oven that has been preheated and then turned off.

Heat 1 generous teaspoon of the oil in a large non-stick frying pan, then turn the heat down to moderate. Spoon a big ladle of batter into the pan. Use the back of the ladle or a spatula to spread the batter over the pan in a circular motion. The batter should not be too thick.

Cook the *dosa* until the underside turns golden, is slightly crisp and does not stick to the pan, about 1–2 minutes. Slide on to a plate, spoon 2–3 tablespoons of stuffing (if using) on one half of the pancake and fold over so that the filling is loosely covered. Wipe the pan and repeat with the remaining batter.

potatoes with cumin seeds
JEERA ALOO

This dish is practically instantaneous if you have leftover cooked potatoes. These spices add a beautiful flavour, bite and depth. Serve with any gravied dish or alternatively, jazz up your favourite roast with this low-fat potato dish instead of roast potatoes. This dish works best with waxy potatoes as floury ones tend to disintegrate.

Serves 2 (quantities can be doubled)

1 tbs vegetable oil
5cm (2 inch) piece of fresh ginger, peeled and cut into fine shreds
1 heaped tsp cumin seeds
½ green chilli, seeded and chopped (optional)
½ tsp turmeric powder
1 rounded tsp coriander powder

2 good pinches each of garam masala and dried mango powder
salt to taste
300g (10½ oz) waxy new potatoes, cooked until tender, peeled and cut into 5cm (2 inch) cubes
1 tbs chopped fresh coriander

Heat the oil in a non-stick frying pan and fry the ginger for 40 seconds. Add the cumin and chilli (if using) and cook for another 30 seconds. Add the remaining dry spices and the salt, stir to combine, then add the potatoes.

Cook on a medium-high heat for 4–5 minutes, stirring often. Try to get a crust on the potatoes. Stir in the fresh coriander and serve hot.

gram flour flat-bread
BESAN KI ROTI

This bread is unusual: it has a nutty flavour and texture, is higher in protein than your average *roti*, and I absolutely love it. If you are following a wheat-free diet it is a great substitute and even if you're not, it is still a treat. If you add the optional extras, particularly the carom seeds, which go especially well with it, this bread is good enough to eat with simple seasoned yoghurt and one of your favourite pickles.

Makes 4–5 breads

130g (4½ oz) gram or yellow chickpea flour (*besan*) plus extra to roll out
½ tsp carom seeds, lightly pounded in a pestle and mortar (optional)
1 heaped tsp dried pomegranate powder (optional)

½ tsp salt
1 pinch of red chilli powder
½ onion, finely chopped (optional)
about 50ml (2 fl oz) cold water to bind
vegetable oil (optional)

Place all the dry ingredients into a bowl, along with the onion (if using), and slowly add water a tablespoon at a time, while constantly mixing and bringing the dough together. You should end up with a soft but not sticky dough.

Heat a *tava* or non-stick frying pan. Divide the dough into 4 or 5 equal-sized pieces, depending on what size bread you want. Take one piece, roll into a ball, dip into the extra flour and flatten with your palm. Roll out into a thin 3mm (⅛ inch) circle 10–13cm (4–5 inches) across.

Dust off the extra flour and slap the bread on to the hot surface of the pan. Cook until the underside has changed colour and comes away easily from the bottom of the pan, about 30 seconds. Turn over and cook the underside until little brown spots appear. If you are using oil, sprinkle a few drops on the bread and spread with the back of a spoon. Repeat the process 2–3 times, turning the bread at 20-second intervals. The whole process should take no more than 1½–2 minutes, and the bread should be golden, with dark spots, and will no longer look matt.

Keep covered while you repeat with the remaining dough.

This dish has no gravy and although it is usually served as an accompaniment it can also be eaten as a pilaff for those of you who want a change. The lentils have a nutty flavour and are slightly al dente rather than mushy. The spices bring out their best without overpowering them. A quick and easy dish to knock up, great for lunch. It even works chilled as a summer spicy outdoor salad.

I often use leftovers to fill samosas (see p. 106) or to stuff breads (see p. 176).

lentil pilaff
SUKHI MOONG KI DAL

Serves 2-3
(quantities
can be
doubled)

100g (3½ oz) (yellow) split mung
    lentils (*dhuli hui moong dal*),
    picked over and washed
1 tbs vegetable oil
½ tsp cumin seeds
4cm (1½ inch) piece of ginger, peeled,
    (2.5cm/1 inch) cut into matchsticks
    and the rest finely chopped
½ small onion, sliced

1 tsp garlic, chopped
1 green chilli, left whole
125ml (4½ fl oz) hot water
salt to taste
½ tsp turmeric powder
¼–½ tsp garam masala
1 tbs lemon juice or to taste
1 small tomato, sliced, and a handful
    of fresh coriander leaves to garnish

Soak the lentils for 20 minutes. Drain.

Heat the oil in a medium non-stick saucepan and stir-fry the cumin and matchstick ginger for 20 seconds. Add the onion and sauté until soft but not coloured, about 5 minutes. Stir in the chopped ginger, garlic and chilli and cook for 30–40 seconds.

Add the lentils, water, salt and turmeric. Bring to the boil, then turn down the heat as low as possible, cover and cook, undisturbed, for 12 minutes. Tilt the pan every so often to make sure the lentils do not catch on the bottom. Uncover and dry off any excess water over a high heat. The lentils should be cooked but still have some texture and bite to them.

Stir in the garam masala and lemon juice. Taste and adjust the seasoning. Garnish with the fresh tomato and coriander. Fluff up with a fork and serve hot.

SOME PEOPLE LOVE them, some people hate them but we all have them. Indians were taught never to throw anything away – everything has nutritional value and food was neither cheap nor abundant. So, leftovers never went to waste; they were either polished off just as they were, or wily, imaginative and proficient mothers would create something new out of them to feed the children.

Personally, I love leftovers. Soups, stews and curries all improve with a day's rest while the flavours develop. I practically always have some leftovers lying around in the fridge. In fact, I make a point of it, as I hate having nothing to eat when I'm hungry. There is also the satisfaction of getting twice the mileage from my time in the kitchen.

LEFTOVERS?

Many impressive meals can be made with leftovers. They need not remind you of the original meal; in fact, their resurgence may be more appreciated than their first appearance. I often transform leftovers by combining them with ingredients and flavours from other cuisines. Samosas can be filled with leftovers from almost any dry dish. Try them with *Potatoes with Onions and Mustard Seeds* (p. 131), *Spicy Peas* (p. 61), *Simply Spiced Spinach* (p. 57), *Tangy Spicy Chickpeas* (p. 145) and *Succulent Creamy Chicken Tikka* (p. 82). Follow the recipe for samosas on p. 106. Spoon leftover *Meatball Curry* (p. 127) over spaghetti, stir any lentil curry into rice for an instant risotto, scatter shredded meat from a leftover curry on to pizza, make a sandwich filling or top toast with – well, with anything, really. I could go on and on as there are so many possibilities for this seemingly humble subject.

Here are a few recipes to get you started. I have not strayed from my Indian roots with these dishes, which will show you how to work leftovers into your favourite meals with surprising results.

chicken biryani
MURGH BIRYANI

A biryani is an aromatic all-in-one rice and meat dish that originally was made with the finest and richest ingredients and the whole process consumed a lot of kitchen time. This version makes use of leftover chicken curry and cooked rice. Easy and tasty, it is an ideal way to use leftovers. I have kept it simple without losing the dish's character. I know you will love it. Serve with yoghurt.

Serves 2 (quantities can be doubled)

300g (10½ oz) leftover *Classic Chicken Curry* (p. 112) or *Cheat's Quick Chicken Curry* (p. 113)
40ml (1½ fl oz) hot water
1 generous tbs low-fat yoghurt
400g (14 oz) leftover cooked rice

2 tsp unsalted butter, chilled
1 good pinch of saffron strands, soaked in 2 tbs hot skimmed milk
a handful of chopped fresh coriander to garnish

Preheat the oven to 180°C/350°F/Gas 4.

Add the hot water and yoghurt to the chicken curry to loosen it a little as the gravy thickens as it cools. Spread 2 spoonfuls of gravy over the base of a small, lidded, ovenproof dish. Spread half the rice over the gravy, then add the chicken and cover with the rest of the rice. Dot the entire surface with small pieces of the butter and drizzle over the saffron milk. Cover with a double layer of aluminium foil and the lid.

Cook in the preheated oven for 20–30 minutes or until the rice and the chicken have heated through. Serve hot, garnished with the coriander.

ambassadorial tandoori chicken sandwich

TANDOORI MURGH KA SANDWICHE

I first had this sandwich at the Ambassador Hotel in Bombay and have never forgotten how good it tasted. This is definitely one of the best sandwiches around. It is now sold in shops and supermarkets all over Bombay and, indeed, London but it won't be as good as this home-made version, especially when you know exactly what is going in it.

Serves 1

2 slices of white bread
1 generous tbs *Green Chutney* (p. 184)
1 heaped tsp low-fat spread,
   margarine or butter
2–3 crunchy lettuce leaves (optional)

salt and freshly ground black pepper
   to taste
60–80g (2–3 oz) shredded *Blond
Tandoori Chicken* (p. 84), reheated

Lightly toast the bread. Spread one slice with the chutney and the other with your choice of spread. Add a layer of lettuce (if using). Season the chicken, pile on to the bread and top with the other slice. Enjoy.

Butter chicken, cooked the traditional way, is a very popular, mild, creamy curry with a hint of sweetness and vast amounts of butter. My version, which uses leftover *Blond Tandoori Chicken* (p. 84), contains only a fraction of the butter, definitely not enough for a starring role. But it is as delicious as the original, which is the type of dish that gets most of us into trouble in the first place. I defy anyone to say that this version leaves them feeling deprived. The paprika adds colour rather than flavour, so leave it out if you prefer. Serve with fresh *naan* (p. 109).

buttery chicken
MURGH MAKHANI

Serves 2 (quantities can be doubled)

200g (7 oz) can peeled plum tomatoes
1 scant tsp fresh ginger, chopped
1 rounded tsp garlic paste
15g (½ oz) raw cashew nuts
1 rounded tsp tomato purée
¼–½ tsp red chilli powder
½ tsp paprika (optional)
salt to taste
½ tsp caster or granulated sugar

125–150g (4–5 oz) leftover *Blond Tandoori Chicken* (p. 84), shredded into large pieces
1 tbs butter
2 tsp dried fenugreek leaves, crumbled
½ tsp garam masala
½ tsp–1 tsp lemon juice or to taste

Pour the tomatoes, ginger, garlic paste and cashew nuts into a small saucepan and boil for 15 minutes, breaking up the tomatoes with the back of the spoon. Add a splash of hot water to keep the mixture loose. Take out the nuts and pound in a pestle and mortar to a fine purée; stir back in, together with the tomato purée, chilli, paprika (if using), salt and sugar. Simmer for 15 minutes, adding hot water when necessary. The gravy should have the consistency of single cream.

Add the chicken and butter. Cook for another 7 minutes over a moderate heat to let the flavours mingle. Add the fenugreek, garam masala and lemon juice. Adjust the seasoning and serve hot.

Buttery Chicken with Naan *Bread*

hot and cold yoghurt rice
DAHI CHAWAL

This simple rice dish, based on leftover rice, is flavoured simply with mustard seeds and curry leaves. The chillies add a touch of heat but should be discarded rather than eaten as they will have you downing a gallon of ice-cream for relief. This is popular in South India where the cooling yoghurt provides a beautiful contrast to the baking heat of the climate and the spicy food. Add any cooked vegetables for extra colour, taste and texture. Serve chilled. Perfect for hot summer days and barbecues.

Serves 1 (quantities can be increased proportionately)

150g (5 oz) cooked rice
4 tbs low-fat yoghurt, beaten
2 tbs semi-skimmed milk
1 tsp vegetable oil
½ scant tsp brown mustard seeds
½ tsp skinned and split black gram (*urad dal*)

7 dried curry leaves
1–2 dried red chillies, whole
1 tsp chopped roasted peanuts (optional)
salt and freshly ground black pepper to taste

Put the leftover rice in a microwave-safe bowl. Cover with a damp napkin and heat for 40–60 seconds on high until hot. Stir in the yoghurt and milk. Allow to cool.

Meanwhile, heat the oil in a small non-stick saucepan and fry the mustard seeds, lentils, curry leaves and chillies until the lentils change colour. Stir into the cooled rice with the peanuts and the seasoning. Allow to cool and refrigerate.

Serve chilled, discarding the chillies.

white cheese in a tomato gravy
PANEER MAKHNI

This dish traditionally uses barbecued (tandoori) cheese but I prefer plain *paneer* as the gravy is wonderfully creamy with the tang of tomatoes and a hint of sweetness. Normally it would contain obscene amounts of cream and butter, but I have kept the fat to a minimum and included some healthier nuts instead of the cream. Great for vegetarians and perfect with *naan* (p. 109). If you don't have a food processor, use a mouli.

Serves 4 with other dishes (quantities can be doubled)

400g (14 oz) can peeled plum tomatoes	½ tsp caster or granulated sugar
2 tsp tomato purée	30g (1 oz) butter
5cm (2 inch) piece of fresh ginger, peeled and roughly chopped	1 tsp vegetable oil
3 fat garlic cloves, roughly chopped	300g (10½ oz) *paneer* (p. 38) made from 2.5 litres (80 fl oz) milk, cubed
40g (1½ oz) cashew nuts	1½ tbs dried fenugreek leaves, crumbled
½ tsp red chilli powder	½ tsp garam masala
1 tsp paprika	2–3 tsp lemon juice or to taste
½ tsp salt or to taste	

Place the tomatoes, tomato purée, ginger, garlic and cashew nuts in a small saucepan and boil for 10 minutes, breaking up the tomatoes with the back of a spoon. Add a splash of hot water to keep the mixture loose. Turn into a food processor and blend until smooth. Add the chilli, paprika, salt and sugar, and simmer for 15 minutes, adding a splash of hot water when necessary. The gravy should have the consistency of single cream. Set aside.

Just before serving, heat the butter and oil in a large non-stick sauté pan. Add the cheese and cook for 4–5 minutes until the cubes develop a slight golden crust. Stir in the gravy and add the fenugreek, garam masala and lemon juice. Taste and adjust the seasoning if necessary. Make sure there is enough gravy in the pan, adding more water from the kettle if necessary; it should be creamy but not thick. Serve hot.

basic stuffed bread
BHARE HUE PARANTHE

These delicious flat-breads can be stuffed with any dry, cooked filling, so are an ideal way to use up leftovers: dry vegetables, lentils or meats. Traditionally they are served with pickles, a bowl of seasoned yoghurt and a large pat of soft fresh butter.

Makes 4

125g (4 oz) chapatti flour (or equal quantities of wholemeal and plain flour), sifted, plus extra for rolling and dusting

around 75–85ml (5–6 tbs) water
8 level tbs dry cooked filling
1½ tbs vegetable oil

Put the flour in a bowl and make a well in the centre. Slowly mix in enough water to make a soft but dry dough. You may not need all of the water.

Knead well until the dough is fairly elastic and forms into a ball. The longer the dough is worked, the softer the bread. Place in a bowl, cover with a damp tea towel and leave in a warm place for 30 minutes.

Keep the dough covered as you make the individual breads. Take a quarter of the dough and knead again to get a smooth tight ball. Flatten slightly and dip both sides into a bowl of the flour. Roll out into a 10cm (4 inch) circle.

Mound 2 level tablespoons of the filling in the centre. Bring up one edge and, working in a circular fashion, bring up the rest of the dough to enclose the filling in a pouch. Pinch the edges together to seal and press down to flatten slightly. Turn over so that the seam is underneath and flatten again. Roll out to a 13–15cm (5–6 inch) round, turning the bread as you go. Make the remaining breads, stacking them between sheets of greaseproof paper.

Heat a *tava* or non-stick frying pan and slap one bread on to the hot surface. Cook, undisturbed, for about 30 seconds or so until the underside has a few brown spots. Turn over and spread ½ a teaspoon of oil over the surface of the bread in a circular motion with the back of a spoon, applying a little pressure. This helps to lightly puff it up. Repeat on the other side. Then continue turning the bread every 20 seconds, without adding more oil, until it is golden with dark brown spots, 1 further minute or so. Repeat with the remaining dough.

This is my favourite *parantha* and I have it at least once a week. The filling is so tasty that I often eat it on its own, using leftover *Simply Spiced Spinach* (p. 57). Like spinach, this bread also combines well with spicy scrambled eggs (see *Indian Omelette*, p. 50). Or go for the traditional accompaniments of seasoned yoghurt, pickles and soft, fresh butter. As an alternative, replace the spinach with leftover *Spicy Peas* (p. 61), *Lentil Pilaff* (p. 167), *Potatoes with Cauliflower* (p. 147) or *Minced Lamb with Peas* (p. 74).

spinach-stuffed bread
PAALAK KA PARANTHA

Enough for 4 breads

450g (1 lb) cooked leftover spinach, or fresh spinach, picked over and washed in at least three changes of water, or frozen spinach
1 tsp vegetable oil
1 tbs garlic, finely chopped
1 tsp fresh ginger, finely chopped

1 tsp cumin seeds
1 tbs dried pomegranate powder
1 heaped tsp coriander powder
½ tsp red chilli powder (optional)
½ tsp garam masala
salt to taste

If using cooked leftover spinach, heat through in a non-stick saucepan, making sure you dry off all excess moisture. If using fresh or frozen spinach, place in a large saucepan with 1 tablespoon of water (fresh only) and cook for about 5 minutes, until completely wilted, or until heated through if using frozen. Drain and refresh under cold water. Squeeze out all the excess liquid and chop finely.

Heat the oil in a non-stick frying pan and gently sauté the garlic, ginger and cumin for 1 minute. Add the spinach and heat through, drying off any excess moisture. If using cooked leftover spinach, add *only* the dried pomegranate powder. If using fresh or frozen spinach, mix in the remaining spices and the salt. Taste and adjust the seasoning if necessary.

Allow to cool. Use to stuff *Basic Stuffed Bread* (opposite).

ACCOMPANIMENTS ARE PREVALENT in every country's cuisine and can be defined as anything that enhances or balances a meal. In India we have four main categories: pickles, chutneys, relishes and yoghurt dishes, and traditionally, a well-laid table would be scattered with a selection of all of them. However, these days we eat differently and may have just one accompaniment or one of each.

Even a simple Indian meal would be presented with a plate of crudités, such as sliced carrots, cucumbers, onions, tomatoes, beetroot and chillies, drizzled with lemon juice and sprinkled with salt and red chilli powder, to add a necessary crunch.

A BIT ON THE SIDE . . .

Yoghurt, eaten at practically every family meal, is the perfect, cool and tangy contrast to Indian food. It can be plain or seasoned, mixed with fried dumplings, practically any vegetable, raw or cooked, herbs or fruits. Once you add something to plain yoghurt, it becomes a *raita* or yoghurt salad. Make these dishes just before serving.

Chutneys can be sweet, savoury or herby. Easy to make, they perk up any meal and are there to provide flavour, unashamedly and unreservedly. Sweet chutneys can rival desserts, and savoury chutneys can be deeper or fresher than the main course. There is space here for only a few of the most common, but the list is endless as any fruit or ingredient can be the basis for a delicious chutney. They are easy to make and usually keep for a week or more in the fridge.

Pickles are very savoury and very spicy. You only need a little to lift the simplest meal. They can be made with any ingredient; the most memorable one I've ever had was a chicken pickle at a roadside restaurant near Delhi.

This classic pickle is very popular for all the right reasons: taste, longevity, great for the stomach and the easiest way to perk up a meal. The flavours are tangy rather than tart as the lemon tenderises and mellows with time, and the sugar takes the edge off the sharpness. The pickle improves with age. In fact, it needs to mature for at least 1 month before you can eat it. It will last for years, kept out of direct sunlight, and a little goes a long way. Indian lemons are smaller and have a thinner skin, which allows the flavours to sink in quickly. Use unwaxed limes or lemons and make sure that you choose fruit with thin skins.

lemon pickle
NIMBU KA AACHAAR

**Makes 450g
(1 lb)**

6 smallish, unwaxed, thin-skinned
  lemons or limes
6 tbs caster sugar
2 tsp black salt (*kala namale*)
4 tsp salt

1 tsp red chilli powder
2 tsp carom seeds
2 rounded tsp freshly ground black
  pepper
2 rounded tsp garam masala

Soak the lemons or limes in water for 2 days. Drain and discard the water.

Cut off the top stalk and the base of 5 of the lemons. Cut into 4 wedges lengthways and slice in half across their width. Squeeze the juice from the remaining lemon.

In a bowl, mix together all the dry ingredients. Add the lemon wedges and, using your hands, work the spice mixture into the segments, squeezing the pieces to extract some juice. Cram into the sterilised jar, together with the juices. Add the juice squeezed from the extra lemon. Seal and shake well.

Leave for at least 1 month (in a northern climate it may take longer). Give the jar a shake every day and, whenever possible, stand it in the sun. Once the fruit skins have turned dark brown, the pickle is ready to eat.

tomato, cucumber and onion yoghurt
TAMATAR, KHEERA AUR PYAAZ KA RAITA

This lightly spiced dish is one of the most common yoghurt salads.
The different textures make it a perfect accompaniment. Serve it as
a cooling summer dip with crudités or *naan* wedges (p. 109).

13cm (5 inch) piece of cucumber,
   peeled
400ml (13 fl oz) low-fat yoghurt,
   chilled and whisked
1 tomato, diced
¼–½ small red onion, diced

salt and freshly ground black pepper
   to taste
½ tsp roasted cumin powder
½ tsp red chilli powder
2 tbs chopped fresh mint or coriander

Serves 4–6

Slice the cucumber lengthways into quarters. Scoop out the seeds and cut the flesh
into 5mm (¼ inch) cubes. Add to the yoghurt with the other vegetables. Season lightly
with salt, plenty of black pepper and cumin powder and stir in the fresh herbs.
Sprinkle over the chilli and serve chilled.

banana raita
KEELE KA RAITA

This yoghurt accompaniment is very refreshing and is perfect for
those of you who like a little sweetness with a spicy meal. Also great
as a healthy mid-afternoon snack or for breakfast.

180ml (6 fl oz) low-fat yoghurt,
   whisked
½ small banana, cut into quarter-moon
   shapes
1 brown cardamom pod, seeds ground
   in a pestle and mortar

1–2 tsp sugar or to taste
a few drops of *kewra* essence or rose
   essence (optional)

Serves 2
(quantities
can be
halved)

Whisk together all the ingredients, chill and serve.

cucumber and mint yoghurt salad
KHEERE KA RAITA

This refreshing dish is great with lamb and chicken, although it goes brilliantly with everything. In the summer I always have a bowl to serve with barbecued meats and vegetables, and spiced potato wedges.

400ml (13 fl oz) low-fat yoghurt, chilled and whisked

13cm (5 inch) piece of cucumber, peeled, coarsely grated and squeezed of all excess moisture

3 tbs fresh mint, shredded

½ tsp roasted cumin powder

½ tsp red chilli powder

salt and freshly ground black pepper to taste

extra fresh mint leaves to garnish

Serves 4–5

Whisk together all the ingredients and serve chilled, garnished with a few mint leaves.

sweet mango chutney
AAM KI CHUTNI

This sweet and sticky chutney provides a wonderful contrast to a hot and spicy meal. Unripe mangoes can be found in Indian grocery stores. This chutney will keep for at least 2 months in the fridge.

300g (10½ oz) raw green mangoes, peeled and grated, yielding just over 125g (4 oz) flesh

½ tsp freshly ground black pepper

½ tsp red chilli powder or to taste

2 fat garlic cloves, grated

4 tbs caster or granulated sugar

2 tbs white wine vinegar

½ tsp garam masala

½ tsp salt

Makes 125ml

(4 fl oz)

Place all the ingredients in a small pan and cook for 8–9 minutes over a moderate heat until thick and sticky. Cool and chill. Pour into a sterilised jar, seal and refrigerate.

sweet and sour vegetable pickle

SABZI KI MEETHI AACHAAR

This tangy pickle is my all-time favourite; I am happy to eat it plain with *roti* (p. 34). It is great served with chicken, meat or a vegetarian meal. If you prefer a savoury pickle, omit the sugar. It is easy to make but takes 1 week to mature and for the flavours to develop. Store when ready to eat in a cool place away from direct light, but do not refrigerate. Once opened, the pickle will keep for 1 month.

Makes 350g (12 oz)

2 medium carrots, peeled and sliced into 7.5cm (3 inch) batons
250g (9 oz) turnips, peeled and sliced into 1cm (½ inch) half-moon pieces
½ small head of cauliflower, washed and cut into florets
2½ tbs white wine vinegar
15g (½ oz) jaggery or soft brown sugar (optional)
½ small onion, cut into large chunks

2.5cm (1 inch) piece of fresh ginger, peeled
2 fat garlic cloves, thickly sliced
2 tbs mustard oil
1½ tbs brown mustard seeds, ground in a pestle and mortar
3 level tsp salt
1–2 tsp red chilli powder
1 tsp turmeric powder
1½ tsp garam masala

Bring a large saucepan of water to a roaring boil. Place the carrots and turnips in a steamer large enough to sit on top of the pan, and steam for 4 minutes. Then add the cauliflower and steam for a further 8 minutes.

Drain the vegetables and dry thoroughly with a tea towel. Dry out further overnight (or longer) in a warm place. (One of the secrets of a good and well-lasting pickle is the complete lack of moisture in the preparation.)

In the morning, check the vegetables. They must be completely dry before continuing with the recipe. If they are still damp, leave them for a longer period.

Heat the vinegar and dissolve the jaggery or sugar in it (if using).

Make a paste of the onion, ginger and garlic, either in a food processor or by grating them finely. Heat the oil in a medium saucepan and fry the paste until golden. Stir in the remaining ingredients, as well as the dried-off vegetables and the vinegar. Mix well.

Pile into a sterilised jar. Cover with muslin and secure with a rubber band. Leave undisturbed, if possible in the sun, for 2 days. Then seal and leave in a dry place for 1 week, shaking at least once a day, and whenever possible exposing it to the sun. It should then be ready to eat.

green chutney
HARA CHUTNI

This highly aromatic and refreshing chutney is served with snacks and barbecued foods. The mixture of the two herbs gives a wonderful rounded flavour. It must be refrigerated and will keep for up to 1–2 weeks without the onion; with the onion, it will only last for 1 week or so. It can also be frozen for at least 1 month. The use of nuts is unconventional but necessary to bind the chutney together, as otherwise it tends to separate: vary the amount of chillies you use, depending on how hot you like your chutney. When serving it, many people add yoghurt to tame the wild flavours a little, especially as a sauce for tandoori foods, but there is no set rule. You will need a food processor.

**Makes
250–300ml
(9–10 fl oz)**

75g (2¾ oz) fresh mint leaves
150g (5 oz) fresh coriander leaves
5g (1 tsp) fresh ginger, peeled and
   chopped
2 cloves garlic, chopped (optional)
1 small onion, chopped (optional)
3–6 green chillies, chopped
15 shelled raw pistachio nuts, ground

1 rounded tsp dried mango powder or
   dried pomegranate powder
2–3 tsp lemon juice or to taste
1 tsp salt
30ml (1 fl oz) cold water
2–4 tbs low-fat yoghurt, to serve
   (optional)

Purée all the ingredients except the yoghurt in a food processor until smooth. Pour into a sterilised jar, seal and refrigerate. If adding the yoghurt, taste the chutney for seasoning and add a little more spice if wished.

quick coconut chutney
JHATTPATTA NARIAL KI CHUTNI

This chutney is absolutely delicious, regardless of whether you like the south Indian fare it normally accompanies. It is quite rich and is served in small portions. The challenge in this recipe is not in making it but in sticking to just the one portion. It is best made with fresh coconut flesh but as I never have one lying around when I need it I started using desiccated coconut which works just as well. If you are south Indian and this is sacrilegious to you, I do not apologise because it tastes like the real thing. Eat on the day you make it.

Makes 3–4 modest servings

1–2 green chillies, seeded and sliced (optional)
1 tsp ginger paste
25g (¾ oz) desiccated coconut
4 generous tbs low-fat yoghurt, beaten
2 tsp vegetable oil
1 tsp brown mustard seeds
8–10 fresh or dried curry leaves
1 tsp each skinned and split black gram (*urad dal*) and split Bengal gram (*channa dal*), picked over, washed and soaked overnight
2–3 dried red chillies (optional)
¼–½ tsp salt or to taste

Pound the green chillies (if using) and the ginger paste in a sturdy pestle and mortar. Add a quarter of the coconut, alternating with a tablespoon of the yoghurt until they are used up and keep pounding until you have a thick rough paste. You can loosen this a little with water for a thinner consistency. Turn into a bowl.

Heat the oil to one side of a small non-stick pan and add the mustard seeds, curry leaves, lentils and red chillies (if using). Fry for 30 seconds.

Stir the pan contents into the coconut mixture, along with the salt, and set aside for at least 30 minutes or until ready to use.

tangy tomato chutney
TAMATAR KI CHUTNI

This simple but delicious chutney is eaten all over the south with just about every meal. I find it perks up the flavours of any chicken or meat dish. The sweetness comes from the caramelised onions and goes wonderfully with the tart and flavourful tomatoes. For a sweeter chutney add sugar to taste. I like to leave it fairly chunky and rustic but it is easily puréed for a more uniform result. It will keep for 3–4 days in the fridge.

Makes 4–5 heaped tablespoons

1½ tbs + 1 tsp vegetable oil
1 medium onion, finely sliced
1cm (½ inch) cube of fresh ginger, peeled and chopped
1–2 dried red chillies, crumbled, *or* ½ tsp red chilli powder
3 garlic cloves, finely chopped

5 medium tomatoes, skinned and diced
½ tsp salt
1 scant tsp brown mustard seeds
7–8 fresh or dried curry leaves
1 scant tsp split and skinned black gram (*urad dal*)

Heat the 1½ tablespoons of oil in a non-stick pan and gently fry the onion until golden brown, about 10–12 minutes. Add the ginger, chillies and garlic and cook for 40–50 seconds.

Add the tomatoes and salt, and cook for 15 minutes over a moderate heat. Keep crushing the tomatoes as you stir, adding splashes of water from the kettle to add liquid to the pan. Reduce to a sloppy purée. Pour into a bowl and set aside.

Wipe the pan clean with kitchen paper. Heat the remaining oil in it and add the mustard seeds, curry leaves and lentils and fry for 30–40 seconds, until the seeds stop sputtering. Stir into the chutney. Serve at room temperature.

Chutneys, clockwise from top right: Tamarind, Tangy Tomato, Quick Coconut, Green

tamarind chutney

IMLI KI CHUTNI

This sweet, fruity chutney has a pleasant tangy undertone. It is served with a variety of snacks and starters, often in combination with seasoned yoghurt. Once opened, it must be refrigerated and will keep for up to 2 months, or it can be frozen for at least 4 months. Adjust the flavourings to suit your taste.

Makes 200ml
(7 fl oz)

400ml (13 fl oz) water
100g (3½ oz) block of tamarind, packed without salt
65g (2½ oz) jaggery or to taste
65g (2½ oz) soft brown sugar or to taste
½ tsp freshly ground black pepper
½ tsp red chilli powder
1 level tsp black salt (*kala namak*)
2 good pinches of salt or to taste
2 level tsp roasted cumin powder
½ tsp garam masala

Bring the water to the boil with the tamarind, and cook over a high heat until the tamarind has broken down and become pulpy, about 25 minutes. Take off the heat and cool.

Once cool place in a colander and drain as much liquid as you can from the fibres, pressing down on them. Return the pan with the resulting liquid to the heat and bring again to the boil. Add the jaggery, sugar, pepper, chilli and salts and cook on a low heat for another 15 minutes.

Add extra water from the kettle if the consistency of the chutney becomes too thick. Stir in the roasted cumin powder and garam masala. Taste and adjust the flavours. If it is too tart, add a little extra sugar. Take off the heat and allow to cool. It thickens as it cools.

Pour into a sterilised jar, seal and refrigerate.

The general rule is the larger the chilli, the milder it is. Here I use large red chillies that are not too hot but the brave-hearted may want to opt for the smaller, more fiery varieties. This pickle is really easy to make and is ideal for when you want to spice up bland dishes. It needs a few days to mature and will keep for 1 month. Refrigerate once opened after which it will keep for 1 further month. Remember to wash your hands thoroughly after making it or wear plastic gloves if you are very sensitive to chillies.

red chilli pickle
LAL MIRCH KI AACHAAR

Fills 1 large jam jar –
450g (1 lb)

2 tbs mustard oil
2 tbs fennel seeds, pounded in a pestle and mortar
2 tsp brown mustard seeds, pounded in a pestle and mortar
1 tbs coriander powder

2 tsp dried mango powder
½ tsp carom seeds
1 tsp salt
12 fat red chilli peppers, washed and stalks removed
1 tsp white wine vinegar

Heat half the oil in a small frying pan, add all the spices and the salt and fry for 30–40 seconds until aromatic, shaking the pan often. Allow to cool.

Slit a pocket in the peppers from top to tail. Scrape out the seeds for a milder pickle. Stuff the cavities tightly with the maximum quantity of spice mixture and place in a small, sterilised jar.

Pour the remaining oil into a small metal ladle or a small saucepan and heat for 1 minute over a high heat, taking care not to burn yourself. Leave to cool.

Cover the chillies with the vinegar and then the oil. Seal the jar. Allow the pickle to mature for 3 days in sunlight or a dry place, shaking every now and again. Refrigerate once opened.

EXPERTS FROM AROUND the world tell us that sugar has little nutritional benefit. I'm willing to bet that most of them had a bar of chocolate in their pocket at the time. Apparently, we are programmed to enjoy sweet foods, so that during our hunter/gatherer days we would seek out fruit to supply our bodies with nutrition and energy. Millennia later, food is hardly scarce but our cravings are still prominent.

Traditionally, Indians sat down to just the one course and no dessert. However, sweet morsels have always been considered auspicious, and religious, festive and happy occasions are 'brightened' with a selection of colourful delicacies. Dinner parties, of course, were the perfect excuse to lay out a sparkling array of sweet dishes to honour and impress as well as feed the guests.

SUGAR AND SPICE

As desserts were usually reserved for special occasions, they were always cloying and indulgent, with small portions satisfying even large cravings. They would be centred around local and seasonal produce such as vegetables, nuts, dried fruit, rice, beans and lentils, which were then enriched with thickened milk, butter, sugar and more nuts. I find it hard to face these puddings (and myself) after a full meal and have lightened the recipes here while maintaining their original character. I promise that you will not be disappointed; they are still glorious and the inherent goodness is an added bonus.

If you are dairy-sensitive, substitute soya milk, which (unless specifically vetoed) when thickened works beautifully in these recipes (see p. 36). The typical Indian garnish of nuts is more than decoration; it adds texture to otherwise 'soft' dishes. I love adding something fruity or crunchy along with the standard Indian offering as an extra texture or to lighten the dish. I have therefore included optional serving ideas on how to prepare fruits with Indian flavourings, as well as a few garnishes to jazz up your puddings.

This Indian version of bread and butter pudding is a party favourite as it is easy to make in large quantities, can be prepared in advance and absolutely everybody loves it. Our pudding is eggless and is made by frying slices of bread in butter and then soaking them in sweetened, thickened milk. I use just enough butter to get the job done while retaining the dish's real character. Leave the crusts on if you like added texture. It's particularly good served with glazed mangoes or peaches (see p. 203).

indian bread pudding
SHAHI TUKRA

Serves 3
(quantities
can be
doubled)

400ml (13 fl oz) can evaporated light milk or 400ml (13 fl oz) *Thickened Milk* (p. 36)
4 tbs caster sugar
seeds of 4–5 green cardamom pods, ground in a pestle and mortar

40g (1½ oz) unsalted butter
2 tsp vegetable oil
2 slices of thick-sliced white bread, cut diagonally into quarters
1 rounded tbs each chopped raw pistachio nuts and slivered almonds

Gently bring the milk to the boil in a small heavy-based saucepan. Reduce by a quarter to 300ml (10 fl oz), about 15 minutes. Add the sugar and cardamom, and stir until the sugar dissolves. Take off the heat and allow to cool. Refrigerate.

Heat a large non-stick frying pan. Melt half the butter and oil, swirl well and once the mixture is foaming, add half the bread, one piece at a time, dipping one side in the fat and then turning it over immediately. Fry until lightly golden on both sides, turning halfway through cooking, 5–6 minutes. Repeat with the remaining fats and bread.

Take the warm bread, dip into the milk and arrange in a shallow serving platter. Allow to cool. Refrigerate.

Remove from the fridge 1 hour before serving and pour over the rest of the milk. It should soak through the bread. Serve at room temperature, garnished with the chopped nuts.

indian rice dreams

PHIRNI

Unlike ordinary Indian rice pudding, this luscious dessert sets a little as it cools, similar to a soft panacotta. Make more than you think you'll eat as there is never enough and as it is so nutritious, a little indulgence won't hurt. *Kewra* essence is a popular flavouring in Indian puddings but you can substitute rose essence or leave it out altogether.

For an elegant dessert, serve in individual bowls, garnished with *Sugared Rose Petals* (p. 205). In winter, use dried apricots that have been soaked and poached in a sugar syrup (equal quantities of sugar and water boiled up together), allowed to cool, then filled with a little of the Rice Dream. Allow 3 per guest, drizzled with sugar syrup and sprinkled with chopped pistachios. Absolutely delicious.

Serves 3 (quantities can be doubled)

- 400g (14 oz) can light (low-fat) evaporated milk
- 125ml (4½ fl oz) skimmed, semi-skimmed or full-fat milk
- 4 level tbs rice flour or long-grained white rice (soaked for 2 hours and processed to a fine paste with 1 tbs water)
- 3–4 tbs caster sugar or to taste
- seeds of 4 green cardamom pods, ground in a pestle and mortar
- 1–2 tbs ground almonds
- 5–6 drops *kewra* or rose essence or 3 tsp rose-water (optional)
- 1 tbs flaked almonds or shelled raw pistachio nuts, roughly chopped, to garnish

Place the milks and the rice flour or processed rice in a heavy-based saucepan and slowly bring to a simmer over a moderate heat, stirring constantly and scraping the bottom of the pan with a metal spoon to make sure the mixture doesn't catch and burn. Once it starts to thicken, lower the heat and cook, stirring, until the pudding has the consistency of thick custard, another 6 minutes.

Stir in the sugar, cardamom, ground almonds and flavouring (if using). Continue to stir until the sugar dissolves.

Remove from the heat and pour straight into a serving dish or individual cocktail glasses. Place cling film directly on to the surface of the *phirni* to stop a skin forming. Refrigerate for 3 hours.

Serve chilled, garnished with the nuts.

carrot halva

GAJAR KA HALVA

This dessert is full of colour, flavour and goodness. In fact, it's actually healthy. Grated carrots are left to languish in a bath of hot milk until tender and enriched. They are then caramelised over a high heat for a full-bodied flavour and texture. Only a little butter is used so that you can leave the table with a smile, satisfied yet innocent. Serve as it is or with *Sweet Saffron Yoghurt* (p. 206) or vanilla ice cream. Alternatively, try it with something sharper and spicier, like cinnamon, cardamom, stem ginger or even citrus fruit ice cream. Do not use soya milk in this recipe as it breaks down the carrots to a pulp.

1 litre (1½ pints) semi-skimmed milk
600g (1 lb 5½ oz) carrots, peeled and
   coarsely grated
1 tbs raisins

6 tbs caster or granulated sugar
   or to taste
1 tbs raw cashew nuts, dry-roasted
   and halved
40g (1½ oz) unsalted butter (optional)

Serves 4

Put the milk in a heavy-based saucepan (non-stick if omitting the butter), bring to the boil then simmer for 10 minutes. Add the carrots and raisins, and cook over a low heat until the milk has dried off, about 50–60 minutes. Stir and scrape the pan (with a wooden spoon if using a non-stick pan) often to prevent the milk from sticking to the bottom and burning.

Stir in the sugar and cashew nuts, mix thoroughly and cook for another 15–20 minutes until the sugar has dissolved and there is no liquid left in the pan. Serve at this point if wished.

Alternatively, add the butter to the pan and cook over a high heat until the carrots have caramelised and darkened. Stir and scrape the bottom of the pan until the mixture comes together, about 15 minutes. Serve hot or at room temperature.

Carrot Halva topped with Jaggery-caramelised Walnuts and Sweetened Yoghurt Cream

trio of 'milk truffles'
THEEN SANDESH

There is no chocolate in these 'truffles' but there is milk, lots of it. *Sandesh* is based on a Gujerati sweet made from puréed *paneer*, a home-made unsalted curd cheese, similar to ricotta. I make the truffles in at least three flavours, stack them in a pyramid and serve them as Indian *petit fours*. These are great candy-like sweets for children and good for them too. Watch out as they can be a little crumbly.

mango 'milk truffles'

AAM KA SANDESH

Here I combine the sweetness of mangoes with nutty coconut. These are really easy to make, and can be prepared in advance.

Makes 8
walnut-size
balls

Flesh of one large mango (see p.20 to prepare)
150g (5 oz) low-fat *paneer* (see p.38)
1–2 tbs icing sugar or to taste

seeds of 2 green cardamom pods, pounded
2 rounded tbs desiccated coconut

Place the mango purée in a small non-stick pan and reduce over a low heat, stirring, until you have 1 scant tablespoon left. Set aside and cool.

Crumble the cheese with the sugar into a medium-sized bowl. Knead with the heel of your hand until you have an even, smooth texture, around 5 minutes. Add the mango purée and cardamom and knead and squeeze until you have a creamy mass. Refrigerate for 10 minutes.

Take rounded tablespoons of the mixture, mould into small balls and roll them in the coconut. Chill until ready but bring back to room temperature to serve.

saffron 'milk truffles'

KESARI SANDESH

These truffles are little balls of summer, flavoured with musty and indulgent saffron and a little orange zest. I roll them in coarsely ground blanched almonds for extra texture.

Makes 8 walnut-size balls

½ tsp saffron strands
1 tbs hot milk (I use the microwave)
2–3 tbs icing sugar or to taste
½ tsp orange zest

150g (5 oz) low-fat *paneer* (see p.38), crumbled
3 tbs almonds, blanched, skinned and finely chopped

Crumble the saffron into the milk. Infuse for 10 minutes. Add the sugar, zest and cheese and knead and squeeze until you get an even, creamy mass, around 5 minutes. Refrigerate for 10 minutes.

Take heaped tablespoons, mould into tight balls and then roll in the almonds. Chill until ready but bring back to room temperature to serve.

turkish delight 'milk truffles'

GULAB SANDESH

Even though these 'truffles' are 100 per cent Indian, they are reminiscent of the rosy flavours of Turkish delights.

Makes 8

150g (5 oz) low-fat *paneer* (see p.38), crumbled
2–3 tbs icing sugar or to taste
5–6 drops rose essence

4 tbs pistachios, finely chopped
sugared rose petals to garnish (see p. 205)

Mix the cheese and sugar and knead and squeeze through your hands until you have an even, creamy mass, around 5–7 minutes. Add the rose essence and nuts. Refrigerate for 10 minutes.

Take heaped tablespoons and roll into small balls. Chill until ready but bring back to room temperature to serve. Place a small sugared rose petal on top.

Kulfi is the Indian version of ice cream but that is really a misnomer as it contains no eggs and no cream. It falls somewhere between an ice cream and a sherbet. It is made with thickened, flavoured milk and is poured straight into either little conical moulds (available at Indian shops; they give you instant portion control, very necessary) or any freezer-proof container. This is a classic recipe to which you can add any flavourings (such as rose essence, orange flower water, saffron) or seasonal fruit purées for variety. Try mango, pomegranate seeds or raspberries. The ground almonds enrich the basic 'cream', rather than add flavour so leave them out if you prefer.

cardamom-flavoured ice cream
KULFI

Makes 6

2 × 400g (14 oz) cans light (low-fat) evaporated milk or 800ml (28 fl oz) **Thickened Milk** (p. 36)
3–4 tbs caster or granulated sugar
2 tbs ground almonds (optional)
1 tsp green cardamom seeds (about 12–14 pods), ground
10 blanched almonds, slivered
1 tbs shelled raw pistachio nuts, chopped
edible silver leaf for decoration (optional)

Bring the milk to the boil in a large heavy-based saucepan, then lower the heat. Reduce by one third, stirring and scraping the base of the pan often to prevent the milk from catching and burning, about 15–20 minutes.

Add the sugar, ground almonds (if using) and ground cardamom and stir until dissolved. The mixture should have the consistency of single cream and be a deep buttery yellow colour.

Take off the heat and allow to cool. Stir in the nuts and decant into the moulds or container. Freeze for at least 5–6 hours. Transfer to the refrigerator for 15 minutes to soften before serving.

To serve, dip the moulds in hot water and turn out, or turn out of the container and cut into slices. Decorate with silver leaf (if using).

rice pudding
KHEER

Indian rice pudding, made with long-grained rice and milk, is one of our most popular desserts. They are cooked together until the milk has thickened and the rice has started to break down, further thickening the dish to give a heavenly dessert with no cream and no butter. It is nutritious as it has carbohydrate, protein, some fat, calcium and plenty of other vitamins and minerals. This is my low-fat version but it is every bit as creamy and satisfying as the original. For a thicker consistency, add a paste of 1 teaspoon of rice flour or cornflour. For a spicy rice pudding, add 2 pinches each of nutmeg and ground cloves, and a quarter-teaspoon of cinnamon powder.

Serves 4–6 (quantities can be doubled)

1.2 litres (2 pints) semi-skimmed milk
1 tbs raisins or golden sultanas
50g (1¾ oz) long-grained white rice, washed
5 green cardamom pods, seeds removed and ground in a pestle and mortar

5 tbs sugar or to taste
2 tbs ground almonds
2–3 drops of rose essence or *kewra* essence, or to taste (optional)
2 tbs chopped almonds and pistachio nuts, to garnish

Bring the milk and raisins to the boil in a heavy-based saucepan. While it is heating, soak the rice in cold water. Add the drained rice and cook, stirring, over a medium heat for 7–8 minutes or until the grains start to plump up and no longer sink to the bottom of the pan.

Lower the heat completely and cook until the rice is tender, around 1 hour. Stir often, scraping the bottom of the pan with a metal spoon to make sure the milk does not catch and burn.

Add the cardamom, sugar, ground almonds and essence (if using). Continue cooking for another 15 minutes, breaking up the rice with the back of the spoon. The pudding should have the consistency of thick custard. It thickens further as it cools.

Allow to cool and refrigerate for 4–5 hours. Serve chilled, garnished with the nuts.

These pan-fried pancakes are an adaptation of the sweet, deep-fried breads that are traditionally eaten with rice pudding in certain seasons. They are chewy with crisp edges and make great accompaniments to the milky, soft desserts in this chapter. You can also serve them with mugs of sweet Indian tea (*chai*, p. 210) at the end of the meal. The longer you leave them after cooking, the crisper they become.

crispy sweet griddle cakes
MEETHA POORA

Makes 12 (quantities can be doubled)

80g (3 oz) plain flour
60–75g (2–2¾ oz) caster sugar
2 brown cardamom pods, seeds removed and pounded in a pestle and mortar
2 tsp fennel seeds, pounded in a pestle and mortar

1 pinch of salt
1 tsp melted butter
125–150ml (4½–5 fl oz) cold water
3 tbs vegetable oil for frying

Mix the dry ingredients in a large bowl. Make a well in the centre, add the butter and most of the water, and stir until you have a thick batter.

Heat the oil in a large non-stick frying pan. Drop tablespoons of the batter into the pan; they will spread slightly. Do not overcrowd the pan. Fry until golden on both sides, about 2–3 minutes per side. Repeat with the remaining batter. There should be enough oil left in the pan to cook all the pancakes. Serve hot, preferably when freshly cooked; alternatively reheat in a hot oven (200°C/400°F/Gas 6), wrapped in foil, for 10 minutes.

jaggery-caramelised walnuts
GUR KE AKROTH

I love these little bites so much that I make them only when I have friends for dinner so that they will finish them off or stop me from doing so. I often use them as a garnish or to add texture to desserts but they also make great, healthy bites for children (jaggery is famous for its health properties). Make sure you use hard jaggery, not the softer version, which is now on the market; it will not work in this recipe. The walnuts are dipped in the carom- and fennel-flavoured jaggery, which solidifies around them to make a fudge-like caramel. They will keep if stored in an airtight container for up to 1 week.

Serves 3 as a nibble or 5 as a garnish for a dessert

100g (3½ oz) hard jaggery
½ tsp carom seeds

½ tsp fennel seeds
80g (3 oz) walnut halves

Pulse the jaggery in a food processor or pound in a pestle and mortar to break it into small pieces. Heat a large non-stick frying pan. Add the jaggery and stir over a low to moderate heat until melted. Stir often and crush up any pieces. When smooth, stir in the carom seeds and fennel, followed by the walnut halves. Stir well to coat them thoroughly. Place each walnut half individually on a sheet of greaseproof paper or on oiled paper or pour the whole lot on to the paper and separate the pieces with two forks. Work quickly as the jaggery will start to harden. If it does, heat the pan a little to melt it again. Leave to cool and harden.

Store in an airtight container.

FRUITS ARE NATURE'S true dessert. India is blessed with a bounty of fruits: apples, small crunchy pears, bananas, pineapples, watermelons, lychees sold on the vine, grapes, small imperfect strawberries, cape gooseberries, dimpled custard apples, papayas, pomegranates, apricots, figs, sweet limes, oranges, huge guavas and other fruits for which I know only the Indian name.

Generally speaking, Indians eat fruits as nature intended: as they are, in the flesh. Occasionally, we sprinkle over a little salt and pepper to bring out the sweetness. Often we juice them for refreshing summertime drinks. We also make fabulous fresh fruit ice creams. But we hardly ever cook them. Fruits are eaten to refresh us, not to warm us up. Even in the colder regions, fruits are always eaten raw.

FRUITS

Fresh fruit may be just what you want after a spicy meal. Create beautiful fresh fruit platters or stack halved raw fruits on a mound of shaved ice. To add a touch of India, serve them with *Cardamom-Flavoured Ice Cream* (p. 198). For a simpler end to a meal, serve ripe fruit with a dollop of *Sweetened Yoghurt Cream* (p. 205), plain, or flavoured with puréed mangoes, or a sprinkling of sweet spices such as cardamom or cinnamon. In the summer, scatter whole strawberries around a bowl of *Sweet Saffron Yoghurt* (p. 206); just dip and enjoy. Top sweet peach halves with a spoonful of *Indian Rice Dreams* (p. 192). For something more complex, try *Spiced Fruits in a Yoghurt Cream* (p. 204).

When cooked, on the other hand, fruits become sweeter and juicier, and pairing them with sweet spices (see below) will further enhance their inherent flavour. Fruit can be grilled, poached, candied, roasted, sautéed, fried – anything really. Here are a few simple recipes to get you started. Use any fruit you love to eat and transform it into something special.

Try a sprinkling of sweet spices or floral essences to enliven any fruit: rose or *kewra* essence or even saffron, cinnamon, clove, nutmeg, mixed spice or fennel seed powders. Indians often pair fruit with stronger spices, and even salt.

cooking fruits

Grilling

Any fruit can be grilled, although some work better than others. The amount of cooking time depends on the grill temperature and the fruit; generally the firmer and denser the fruits, the longer they require. Some soft fruits, such as berries, grapes, figs, oranges or very ripe fruit, can be sweetened, flavoured with a few of the spices or essences mentioned opposite, wrapped in double foil and heated just long enough to burst their skins and release their juices. Throw whole bananas in their skins under the grill and roast until black all over and the flesh is meltingly soft. Split open and top with *Cardamom-Flavoured Ice Cream* (p.198) or yoghurt. Sprinkle pineapple, apricots, peaches, plums, dates, mangoes, etc., with a few spices or flavourings and a dusting of white or brown sugar. Place straight on an oiled grill or griddle pan and cook until caramelised.

Glazing

Glazing fruit is one of the simplest yet most elegant things you can do with it. There is one caveat, however: the fruit has to be sweet and ripe enough to speak for itself. Halve your chosen treasure, sprinkle the cut half with caster sugar and caramelise with either a culinary blowtorch (it takes seconds) or flash under a preheated grill. Allow the sugar to melt and turn golden before serving individually on a plate alongside a scoop or dollop of your choice. I love to serve glazed fruits with *Indian Bread Pudding* (p. 191) or *Sweet Saffron Yoghurt* (p. 206).

Poaching

Poaching is a simple technique of cooking and softening fruit in a sweet liquid. The flavours of the poaching syrup permeate the fruit and infuse it with its own character. It can be flavoured with anything: wine, fruit juices, floral extracts, or, of course, spices. Use fruits that are soft but will hold their shape once cooked. Poached pears and peaches are two of my favourites, which both marry well with sweet spices.

Peel the pear; leave the peach with its skin on. Poach them in the syrup used in the recipe on p. 204 until soft when poked with a cocktail stick or the tip of a knife. Remove with a slotted spoon. Reduce the poaching liquor over a high heat until it is syrupy. To serve, peel the peach; the skin should be soft and come away easily. Cut a small slice off the base of the pear so that it stands upright. Serve with your choice of accompaniment and a good drizzle of the syrup.

This dessert is light and refreshing, ideal after a heavy meal. Either the syrup or the whole dish can be prepared in advance and refrigerated until serving, although it tastes better if removed from the refrigerator 15 minutes beforehand. Use any seasonal fruits, cut into large, presentable pieces (I use four of the larger fruits and several of the smaller ones). Place them on a platter, pour over the syrup and let everyone help themselves. I like to serve this with a dollop of *Sweetened Yoghurt Cream (p. 205)* as I find it is the perfect tart contrast to the sweet fruit.

spiced fruits in a yoghurt cream
PHAL AUR DAHI KI MALAI

4 portions prepared fruits, such as
  apple, pear, plum, peach, apricot,
  pineapple, mango, lychee, papaya,
  orange, grape, pomegranate, melon
flaked almonds, toasted, to serve

SYRUP
80g (3 oz) jaggery or 3–4 tbs soft
  brown sugar to taste
400ml (13 fl oz) cold water
3 green cardamom pods, lightly
  pounded to open

2 brown cardamom pods, lightly
  pounded to open
7.5cm (3 inch) cinnamon stick or
  ⅓ tsp cinnamon powder
3 cloves or ½ tsp ground cloves
2.5cm (1 inch) piece of fresh ginger,
  peeled and sliced thinly
2–3 drops of rose essence or
  1 tbs rose-water
2–3 black peppercorns

Serves 4

Place all the ingredients for the syrup in a small saucepan and stir over a low heat until the sugar completely dissolves. Bring to the boil, then simmer for 10 minutes or until thickened and syrupy. Pour straight over the prepared fruit.

Garnish with the nuts and serve with *Sweetened Yoghurt Cream*.

sweetened yoghurt cream
MEETHI DAHI KI MALAI

I always have some Greek yoghurt in the fridge as it keeps for ages and is very versatile. It may not be an Indian ingredient but I often find myself serving a dollop with hot sweet Indian puddings for a cool and tangy contrast. Try it with hot *Carrot Halva* (p. 194) or warm grilled fruit.

200g (7 oz) Greek yoghurt (any fat content)

icing sugar to taste
½ tsp lemon or orange zest

Whisk together and chill.

variation
You can transform this refreshing accompaniment by adding a couple of tablespoons of desiccated coconut to the yoghurt.

sugared rose petals
MEETHI GULAB KI PAKHRI

These make a wonderful edible garnish for desserts.

1 egg white
pink rose petals (organically grown)

caster sugar

Lightly whisk the egg white. Using a soft brush, coat both sides of each rose petal lightly with egg white and dip in the caster sugar. Shake off any excess. Leave to set for 2–3 hours in a dry place.

sweet saffron yoghurt
SHRIKAND

Shrikand is a thickened and sweetened yoghurt flavoured by and coloured with saffron. The alchemy of the saffron with the yoghurt transforms it into something much less innocent. This dessert is perfect for dinner parties. It is easy to make, can be prepared in advance and is a perfect, light, refreshing ending to any meal. Try serving it in tall martini glasses with the rims moistened and then dusted with powdered pistachio nuts. Alternatively, present on an attractive plate, scattered with *Sugared Rose Petals* (p. 205), or serve with plenty of ripe strawberries for dipping.

Serves 4–6

1 litre (1½ pints) low-fat yoghurt
½ tsp saffron strands
2 tsp hot milk
5–6 tbs icing sugar or to taste
seeds of 5–6 green cardamom pods, crushed

1 tbs rose-water or 2–3 drops of rose essence
1–2 tbs shelled raw pistachio nuts, chopped, for garnish
edible silver leaf for decoration (optional)

First, thicken the yoghurt. Line a large sieve with muslin or cheesecloth. Place over a bowl, pour in the yoghurt and refrigerate overnight, letting the whey drip away. Discard the whey the following day.

Crumble the saffron strands into the hot milk and infuse for 5 minutes, stirring and occasionally crushing with the base of a spoon.

Beat the sugar, cardamom, saffron milk and rose essence into the thickened yoghurt. Allow to cool and refrigerate for 3 hours.

Serve chilled, garnished with the nuts and silver leaf or a sugared rose petal (if using, p. 205).

DRINKS

ALL INDIAN DRINKS have a purpose. They are either meant to refresh the sun-drenched population, to revive those tired from a day of work, to warm up the blanketed masses or to relieve a mild ailment. The ones we drink to refresh us are often slightly salted as well as sweet to help replace minerals lost through dehydration, whereas those used to heat and perk up the body in winter are lightly flavoured with spices to warm, stimulate or relax.

One of India's best-known exports is *chai*, spiced brewed tea, and to be honest it really is the best thing since sliced bread. The milk is heated with the water and infused with a selection of sweet spices, often including ginger for a warming and stimulating effect (see p. 211). A lesser-known fact is that coffee is as popular in the south as tea is in the rest of India. south Indian coffee is famous in its own right and is exported as is tea. Both are consumed in small quantities and are thick and sweet.

The drinks in this chapter are all based upon authentic recipes that have been adapted to suit modern lifestyles. The drinks vary from simply refreshing to complex and memorable. All are delicious and, more importantly, thirst quenching. Some are so good that they double as a dessert and are nutritious enough to have for breakfast. They can all be sweetened and spiced according to personal taste.

This may not sound very Indian, but it is eaten (or drunk) all over India. As far as I am concerned, no authentic Indian cookbook would be complete without it. This luscious milky concoction is ideal at any time on a hot day. Normally, it is served in a tall glass topped with a scoop of creamy vanilla ice cream, which seductively melts into the coffee. Everything in this recipe is low-fat, but it is still a real treat. I make it with instant coffee but if you have a good coffee machine use your favourite brand. Remember when adding the sugar that there is sweetness in the ice cream.

cold coffee with low-fat ice cream
THANDA COFFEE AUR ICE CREAM

Serves 2
(quantities
can be
doubled)

2 tsp instant coffee, dissolved in a tiny
    amount of hot water
300ml (10 fl oz) semi-skimmed milk
2–3 tsp caster or icing sugar or
    to taste

2–3 ice cubes
2 small scoops low-fat vanilla
    ice cream, to serve

Put the coffee, milk, sugar and ice cubes in a food processor and give them a quick whizz to break up the ice and create the lightest froth. The longer you blend it, the frothier it becomes, needing a little time to settle. If you don't have a food processor, crush the ice by putting it in a freezer bag and smash it with a rolling pin. Stir the coffee, milk and sugar together until the sugar has completely dissolved. Stir in the ice.

Pour into tall glasses and top with the ice cream. Serve with a spoon.

tea

CHAI

This home-made brew is a far cry from the new-wave milky *chai* drinks sold in the national coffee chains. This is authentic Indian tea, as served all over India at roadside tea-stalls. A serving is poured into a metal cup with the required amount of sugar and then expertly mixed by pouring it from one cup to another from a height sufficient to dissolve the sugar. The end-result is nectar. The quality of the tea does not have to be superior (I use a standard blended tea bag). The downside of real *chai* is that many Indians don't enjoy tea when outside India or their own homes.

Makes 1 mug (quantities can be doubled, trebled, etc.)

200ml (7 fl oz) cold water
100ml (3½ fl oz) semi-skimmed milk
granulated sugar to taste

1 tea bag or 1 tsp tea leaves of your preferred blend

Bring the water, milk and sugar to the boil. Simmer for 1 minute. Add the tea and simmer gently, 1 further minute for a tea bag and a little longer for tea leaves. Take off the heat and strain into a large mug.

cardamom tea

ELAICHI CHAI

This tea, a simple variation of ordinary *chai*, is what most Indians drink. Break 1 pod per person and add with the milk.

indian spiced tea
CHAI MASALA

Chai is the Indian word for tea. It has recently become popular in trendy coffee bars across the country, a blend of milk, tea and spices. However, delve a little deeper and this Western brew and our own are continents apart. Indian tea is strong and rich with spices adding an extra heat that has nothing to do with temperature. We brew the tea, milk and spices together in a saucepan until it evolves to the perfect combination. This recipe was given to me by a family friend. It makes a brilliant cuppa.

4 tsp fennel seeds
4 brown cardamom pods, seeds only
8 green cardamom pods, seeds only
2 whole cinnamon sticks

8 cloves
1 tsp powdered ginger
½ tsp freshly ground black pepper
   or 4 black peppercorns

Grind together and store in an airtight container.

spiced ginger tea

ADRAK MASALA CHAI

This tea is the ultimate in brewed tea and by far my favourite. Infused with spices and ginger, it is warming and comforting at any time of the year. Ginger and fennel are known to aid digestion, so this tea is great after a heavy meal. Add a few thin shavings of fresh ginger to the brewing tea and $1/4$ tsp of tea spices to taste.

north indian flavoured buttermilk
NAMKEEN PUNJABI LASSI

Lassi is practically a national drink. It is drunk by children in the morning and by their fathers in the afternoon to cool off after hot laborious days. Buttermilk, a by-product of making butter, is very low in fat and great for digestion, with a very subtle flavour. Buttermilk is not always easy to find so I often use equal quantities of yoghurt and water instead. It gives the same result. Many Westerners are unused to savoury beverages, but once you give this refreshing and extremely nourishing drink a try you will soon be hooked.

Serves 1–2 (quantities can be doubled)

400ml (13 fl oz) low-fat buttermilk or
   200ml (7 fl oz) each low-fat yoghurt
   and cold water whisked together
1 good pinch of salt
2 good pinches of roasted cumin
   powder

1 tbs chopped fresh coriander
   (leaves and stalks)
1 tbs chopped fresh mint leaves
freshly ground black pepper

Whisk all the ingredients together until a little frothy. Serve chilled with crushed ice.

south indian flavoured buttermilk
NAMKEEN MADRASI LASSI

These refreshing drinks can be flavoured with any ingredient but while sweet versions are now found infused with floral essences and thickened with fruit purées, their savoury counterparts have stayed close to the original. This vibrant version is enlivened with the subtle use of typical southern Indian flavours and is a must-try if you like the humble *lassi*.

½ tsp vegetable oil
½ tsp brown mustard seeds
3 fresh or dried curry leaves, shredded
1 good pinch of salt
1 pinch each of red chilli powder and
   turmeric powder

400ml (13 fl oz) low-fat buttermilk or
   200ml (7 fl oz) each low-fat yoghurt
   and cold water whisked together

Heat a tiny amount of vegetable oil in a non-stick saucepan. Add the spices. Once the seeds stop spluttering, take off the heat and pour in the buttermilk. Stir well to combine and pour into a glass. Allow to cool and refrigerate. Serve chilled.

sweetened buttermilk
MEETHI LASSI

Sweet *lassi* is one of the best ways to refresh yourself during the long hot summer months in India. Plain and flavoured buttermilk drinks are fast gaining popularity in Britain and can be bought in coffee bars and supermarkets, but it is so easy to make fresh at home. They are comparable to a thin yoghurt milkshake and can be tailored to suit your mood and the season. Add puréed fruits or other flavourings to the basic recipe.

400ml (13 fl oz) low-fat buttermilk or
   200ml (7 fl oz) each low-fat yoghurt
   and cold water

1–2 tsp caster or icing sugar or to
   taste
2–3 drops of rose or *kewra* essence
   (optional)

Whisk together all the ingredients until frothy. Serve chilled with ice.

mango sherbet
AAM KI LASSI

The sweet warmth of the mango works wonderfully with the tangy buttermilk in this highly refreshing drink. Also great for breakfast.

Serves 2
(quantities
can be
doubled)

1 large ripe raw mango
400ml (13 fl oz) low-fat buttermilk or
  200ml (7 fl oz) each low-fat yoghurt
  and cold water

1–2 tbs caster or icing sugar or to taste

Remove the flesh from the mango (see p. 21), making sure you capture all the juice. Process together with the remaining ingredients and serve with ice. Alternatively, press the mango flesh through a sieve and whisk with the remaining ingredients. For a thicker consistency, use less water and add more mango to taste.

sweet and spicy lemon water
SHIKANJI

This lemony drink is absolutely delicious and highly refreshing. It is our version of lemonade. The addition of the salt and pepper is traditional and helps counter dehydration.

Serves 2
(quantities
can be
doubled)

500ml (18 fl oz) cold water
juice of 1 large lemon
3 tbs caster sugar or to taste

½ tsp black or ordinary salt
½ tsp freshly ground black pepper

Combine all the ingredients and stir together until the sugar has dissolved. Serve chilled with crushed ice.

Drinks, clockwise from top right: Sweet and Spicy Lemon Water, South Indian Flavoured Buttermilk, Mango Sherbet, North Indian Flavoured Buttermilk

FOOD GLOSSARY

This is intended as a brief explanation of the ingredients and foods used in the recipes in this book. For newcomers to Indian cuisine, there is a whole world waiting to burst into your kitchen.

asafoetida *heeng*
A beige-coloured resin (often bought in powder form), known to aid digestion as well as to cleanse and strengthen the digestive system. Use in pinches as it is very strong.

bay leaf *tej patta*
A dried, flat leaf, used to flavour sauces and curries.

beans
Beans are the edible parts of leguminous plants. They are full of vitamins and minerals and, when combined with a grain or dairy product, form a complete protein. Buy them dried, fresh or canned. Dried beans must be rinsed and soaked to render them more digestible (see p. 22). When whole beans are split, they are referred to as lentils (see p. 22).

chickpea *kabuli channa/cholle* Also known as garbanzo. A hazelnut-like legume with a meaty, nutty flavour.

mung bean *sabut moong* A small green oval bean that is very important in Indian food. It can be found whole, split and ground as flour. Indians also sprout them to use in nutritious spiced salads (see p. 23).

red kidney bean *rajma* A full-bodied, kidney-shaped, burgundy-coloured bean.

whole Bengal gram *kaala channa* A medium-sized, robust brown bean with an earthy flavour, also known as a black chickpea and similar in appearance to black gram. A very important ingredient in Indian cooking. Look for it in Asian markets.

black salt *kala namak*
Black salt is a spicy, dirty-looking salt, which I have only ever seen in Indian cooking. It can be found in Indian stores. Although there is no real substitute as it is highly aromatic, use salt and pepper if unavailable.

bottle gourd *ghiya*
Bottle gourd, also known as *dudhi* and *lauki*, is a long, pale green vegetable gourd. It has a fresh character and mild flavour.

buttermilk
Buttermilk, a by-product of the butter-making process, is a thin, slightly tart liquid that is naturally low in fat, resembling milk. It is normally drunk before a meal or on a hot day to cool the body. Buttermilk is said to help digestion and is very important in Ayurvedic food.

cardamom pods *elaichi*
There are two main types used in Indian food: large brown pods and smaller green ones. Both are used whole to flavour curries and pilaffs, as well as in garam masala. The seeds are often ground and can be found in savoury and sweet dishes. Cardamom is believed to aid in digestion, improve absorption and help the spleen to function properly.

carom seeds *ajwain*
A dark green seed with a firm character. It is very flavourful and small quantities do the trick. Known to be good for the stomach.

chaat
Chaat is the term given to any cold, spicy salad, made with either vegetables or fruit. It can be simple, comprising only one ingredient, or complex and topped with yoghurt and chutneys. With or without all the trimmings, *chaat* is a healthy way to ease those between-meals hunger pangs.

chaat masala

A special spice mix often sprinkled over street foods and snacks for an extra-spicy kick. It can be found in Indian stores. If unavailable, substitute with garam masala and a little dried mango powder.

channa masala

A wonderful spice mix prepared especially for chickpea dishes, sold in ethnic stores. It will transform any chickpea dish in an instant.

chapatti flour *atta*

A fine-textured flour used to make *rotis*. It can be found in Indian stores, but if unavailable substitute with equal quantities of plain and wholemeal flour.

chillies *mirch*

Whole chillies add more to a dish than just heat; they also add a distinct flavour that would be missed if omitted. Red chillies are ripened green ones and are equally hot. They contain the phyto-chemical capsaicin, which has powerful antioxidant properties, helps to stimulate the digestion and metabolism, and cleanses the colon of toxins. The seeds and membrane inside the chilli carry most of the heat; the colourful flesh provides the aroma and flavour. For flavour without the heat, use the chillies whole and discard them when the dish is ready, or slit and scrape away the seeds. Also bear in mind that the strength of chillies varies from one batch to the next, so always check by either tasting the chilli or by adding it a little at a time.

Indians use both fresh and dried chillies. You can find many varieties of chillies with a spectrum of heat, but we mainly use long slim fresh ones and small dried red chillies, which look shrivelled but are very hot. The general rule is the smaller the chilli, the bigger the bite. If you don't have either type on hand, use chilli flakes or powder instead. Many of these recipes stipulate chilli powder as it is widely accessible but if you have fresh chillies, use these for an authentic flavour.

Be careful when handling chillies as they can irritate the more delicate areas of the skin as well as the eyes. Always wash your hands properly or wear plastic gloves when handling them. If you bite into a chilli and your mouth is on fire, drink iced water, or eat yoghurt or something sugary.

cinnamon *dal cheeni*

Cinnamon is a naturally sweet spice that most of us are familiar with. It is believed to increase digestive assimilation, stimulate the kidneys and help with the absorption of nutrients. It does not keep well, so buy in small quantities.

cloves *laung*

Cloves are the highly aromatic dried flowers of the clove tree. The spice is fragrant and a touch sweet. Cloves and clove oil are often used to alleviate common cold symptoms, and in India people still bite on a clove to ease a throbbing toothache.

coconut milk powder

You can buy this in most supermarkets, where it is usually to be found near the Oriental products. It is actually powdered coconut milk. I use this versatile product instead of fresh or canned coconut milk as there is no wastage. Add a little extra for a more concentrated flavour of the tropics.

colocasia *arbi*

These starchy root vegetables are similar to yams and potatoes but with their own distinctive flavour. Look for them in Indian markets.

coriander leaves *hara dhania ka patta*

Coriander is integral to Indian cuisine and is mentioned in texts 7,000 years old. Its parsley-like leaf is refreshing and aromatic. According to the ancient Indian science of Ayurveda, coriander relieves indigestion and improves digestive power, as well as alleviating allergies and rashes. Fresh coriander can be washed and stored in fresh water in the refrigerator for one week, or frozen for up to one month in an airtight container. This herb loses its character when dry, so use fresh or frozen. Coriander is more than a garnish; it adds a lot of flavour to a dish.

coriander seeds and powder *sabut aur pisi hui dhania*

These seeds are one of the defining spices of Indian food. Mild and aromatic, they are known to have a cooling effect on the body, and are particularly good for the digestion and absorption of nutrients. Before grinding the seeds, first roast until fragrant.

cumin seeds *jeera*

These resemble caraway seeds, except that they are a lot more savoury. Indians mainly use 'white' cumin, which is actually brown in colour. Cumin increases digestion and absorption and is useful for digestive disorders. Cumin powder is powdered raw cumin. Roasted cumin powder is powdered cumin that has already been roasted (p. 22).

curry

Curry is a purely British term, which in essence refers to a gravied dish.

curry leaves *kari patta*

These have nothing to do with curry. They are the small, green and very flavourful leaves of the neem tree and are used abundantly in south Indian cooking, either fresh or dried.

curry powder

Curry powder is the Western term given to a spice mix made from Indian spices. However, no such spice mix is used in India. Every household blends an individual mix to flavour food. I would never use a commercial curry powder as everything just tastes like a 'curry-house' dish.

drumsticks

A long, tubular vegetable grown and eaten in south India (where they are often used to make curries and pickles), with a fibrous inedible skin and sweet flesh. They can be found canned in Indian shops in the UK. Best eaten with the fingers and chewed to release their soft and juicy flesh. Discard the woody exteriors.

fennel seeds *saunf*

A slender, green seed with a mild aniseed flavour. Delicious in food and also known for its digestive properties. Roasted fennel seeds are often passed around in India after dinner as they help to digest the meal and act as a mouth freshener.

fenugreek leaves *methi aur kasturi methi*

Highly savoury, this dark-leaved herb adds tremendous flavour to a dish. Use fresh or dried. You may find yourself wanting to add them to everything.

fenugreek seeds *methre*

These flat, beige seeds can be a little bitter and are normally used sparingly to impart their unique flavour to dishes. Fenugreek seeds are credited with a wealth of healing properties; they are nourishing, aid digestion and alleviate allergies.

garam masala

This spice mix is used in practically everything. Recipes vary from one household to the next and even the brands in the markets differ in strength, so always taste to check the spiciness. However, freshly ground garam masala is hard to beat. For my recipe see p. 31.

garlic *lasan*

This popular member of the onion family transforms even the blandest dish into something delightful. As a bonus, it is one of nature's healthiest foods. It is believed to help lower blood pressure, prevent blood clots, reduce 'bad' cholesterol and neutralise harmful free radicals. The longer you cook garlic, the milder it becomes.

ghee

Ghee is the Indian name for clarified butter, which can be used to cook food at high temperatures without burning. It is more expensive than oil in India, where it is considered a premium product. Many people avoid ghee because of its saturated fat while many practitioners of Ayurveda believe it is very beneficial for the body.

ginger *adrak*

Ginger, a fibrous rhizome, is fresh and sharp at the same time. This power-packed food is believed to help digestion, alleviate gas and cramps, and relieve the symptoms of a cold. It is also known to help ease morning sickness and general nausea, and to reduce 'bad' cholesterol. Buy fresh root ginger with smooth skin and peel before using. You can freeze peeled ginger and grate it straight from frozen. You can also make a ginger paste (see p. 30) and freeze in teaspoon-size portions to pop straight into the pan.

gram flour/yellow chickpea flour *besan*

A key ingredient in Indian cookery. It is used to bind ingredients; to make batters, flat-breads and dumplings; and to flavour vegetables. It is flour made not from the chickpea itself but from a relative (see Bengal gram, below). It is yellow in colour and can be found in any Indian shop and many supermarkets.

halva

Halva is a generic term used to describe a certain type of dessert, rather like an English 'pudding', and can be made with grains, lentils, vegetables or fruit. It is normally quite soft and texture is added with nuts. The only rule is that it has to be sweet.

jaggery *gur*

A flavourful, unrefined dark sugar, which is renowned for its health properties. It has an unusual caramel flavour. Jaggery can be bought in Indian stores, keeps well and can be used to sweeten anything. There are two types: hard jaggery and now a soft version, which has been specially treated. I prefer to use the harder, more authentic block of jaggery. If unavailable, palm sugar (soft brown sugar), a natural unrefined sugar from palm trees, can be a good substitute.

kewra essence

This flavouring is extracted from the screw pine plant and is often used to perfume Indian puddings.

lentils *dal*

Lentils are peas and beans that have been split and sometimes skinned. Indians eat a large variety of lentils, many of which are just finding their way into Western supermarkets. As they are still new in Britain you may have to go to Indian shops to find them, so I list both the lentil's Indian name as well as its Anglicised name to avoid confusion. They are full of goodness with vitamins, minerals and fibre, and are a good combination of both carbohydrates and protein. They keep well in airtight containers away from direct light.

Bengal gram *channa dal*

Similar to the yellow split pea, Bengal gram is the split and skinned variety of a dark-skinned, yellow-fleshed chickpea. It is nuttier than the beige chickpea and is very common in Indian cuisine from the north to the south.

mung lentil *moong dal*

These lentils come from mung beans and have a green skin and a cream interior. They have an earthy flavour and a nutty texture. Indian stores always stock them split or 'broken', as well as whole; otherwise you can split them yourself by pulsing whole mung beans in a food processor.

yellow skinned, split mung bean *dhuli hui moong dal*

The skinned version of the split mung bean is yellow with a mild, buttery flavour. They are one of the most popular lentils and are considered the easiest to digest.

black gram, whole *ma ki dal* and skinned *dhuli hui ma dal*

These small black beans have a creamy but deep flavour and are used both whole and split with the skins off. When 'broken', they show their light beige meat and have a nuttier character.

red lentil *masoor dal*

A salmon-coloured lentil with a smooth taste and a creamy texture.

split pigeon pea *arhar/toovar dal*

These peas produce shiny, ochre-coloured lentils. They have a nutty texture and are often sold coated in a protective oil that must be washed off before use.

lotus root *bheh*

Lotus root is a fibrous root vegetable with a crunchy texture. The tough brown skin has to be removed before cooking. Look for fresh produce in Oriental or Indian shops; otherwise frozen or canned versions work just as well.

mace *javitrii*

Mace is the bright scarlet membrane that surrounds the nutmeg. It is dried and sold whole (known as blades) and ground. A little goes a long way and really complements meat dishes.

maize flour

This is made from yellow corn and is used to thicken food or to make breads; its texture is coarser than the white cornflour more often used for the same purpose in the West.

mango powder, dried *amchoor*

This light beige powder, made from unripe mangoes, adds a tart and tangy flavour to a dish. If unavailable, substitute lemon juice.

mustard oil *rai ka thel*

A pungent oil, which is used quite often in Indian food as it has a powerful flavour and is cheaper than other oils. It is the only oil used in pickle making.

mustard seeds *rai aur sarson*

There are three types of mustard seeds. The yellow ones, used to make Western mustard, are seldom found in Indian cooking. The black ones (*sarson*) are used to make mustard oil and are quite mild when cooked. The brown ones (*rai*) are a defining ingredient in south Indian food and impart a distinctive, slightly tart flavour.

nigella onion seeds *kalonji*

Small black, teardrop-shaped seeds with a pungent, peppery flavour.

paneer

An unsalted, white, home-made cheese similar to Italian ricotta but much firmer. It has a bland flavour and a very fresh taste. Purists eat it sprinkled with roasted spices and a squeeze of lemon juice, but it is delicious in any dish and soaks up the flavours paired with it. For my low-fat recipe, see p. 38. If unavailable use tofu instead.

pao bhaji masala

This special spice blend is always used when making the dish of the same name, which I call *Six Veg and a Couple of Rolls* (p. 76). It is absolutely delicious. It can be found in most Indian stores, is inexpensive and keeps for one year.

papri

Papri are best compared to thick round potato crisps but made with flour. They have a great crunchy texture and their own subtle flavour. In India *papri* form part of a street-side snack, which is made with boiled potatoes, chickpeas and yoghurt. They also make great canapé bases for myriad toppings. You can often buy *papri* in Indian stores but they are easily made at home (see p. 46).

pilaff *pullao*

A pilaff is a general term for a spiced rice dish.

pomegranate seeds, dried *anardana*

These dark seeds of the pomegranate fruit were introduced to Indian food from Persia. They are now commonly used to flavour and add tartness to a dish. See p. 20 for instructions on how to make dried pomegranate powder or buy it ready made.

quorn

Quorn is a recent addition to vegetarian protein ranges. It is made from mushrooms and egg white and is high in protein and low in fat. It comes either in chunks or as mince, and can be found in the chilled or frozen sections in supermarkets. If unavailable substitute soya products.

raita

Once any ingredient has been added to plain yoghurt (fruits, vegetables, dumplings or just spices) it becomes a *raita*.

rose essence

This delicate essence is extracted from rose petals and is used to flavour desserts and drinks. It is stronger in flavour than rose-water.

saambar powder

A blend of spices, abundantly used in south Indian cuisine, which can be found in Indian stores.

saffron *kesar*

Saffron is the dried stamens of the crocus flower. This spice is used sparingly, as it is very expensive and strong. The strands give food a vibrant, yellow-orange colour and a distinct musky flavour.

samosa

A triangular-shaped pastry filled with a choice of meat and vegetable fillings. Traditionally, they are deep-fried. I use filo pastry and bake them, with a lighter and more digestible result.

silver leaf *vark*

On festive occasions, Indians often garnish dishes with a very thin film of edible silver leaf. It is sold in Indian stores in sheets and is easy to use.

soya milk

An emulsion of soya beans and water, which is often substituted for cow's milk. It is available sweetened, plain or with added vitamins, is vegan and contains no lactose. Soya milk can be used instead of cow's milk in all the recipes here and, in fact, tastes absolutely amazing when thickened (see p. 36) and used in desserts.

tamarind *imli*

Tamarind is prized for its fruity sourness and is especially popular in South Indian cuisine. Fresh tamarind pods look like knobbly fingers with a brown papery skin. The flesh is attached to large seeds inside and the flavour has to be coaxed from the fruit. In the West, tamarind is often sold in large blocks (packed either with salt or without) from which pieces are cut off to extract the juice (see p. 27). Tamarind is also sold as a paste, or in concentrate form. I find this too strong so I suggest you stick with the paste or block variety.

tandoori cooking

A *tandoor* is a barrel-shaped clay oven and its results are so popular that a whole cooking style has been named after it. The temperature in a *tandoor* can reach 287°C/550°F, cooking food in a very short time without drying it out. These ovens are mainly found in restaurant kitchens, so to make tandoori food use a barbecue, grill or griddle pan, or a very hot oven.

tarka

Tarka is the Indian term for tempering, where a few basic ingredients are cooked in hot oil and stirred into a dish at the end of the cooking process for a fragrant punch of flavour.

turmeric powder *haldi*

This yellow spice is used for its flavour, colour and healing properties; it is believed to encourage a good metabolism, purify the blood and disinfect wounds.

Indian Product Sources

I am sure all of you have a local Indian shop somewhere around the corner or, in indeed, on the corner. I highly recommend a visit just to see the range of interesting spices and products that are on your doorstep. I always get lost in these shelves, my eyes taking in unfamiliar products or packaging while I search for the items on my list. However, many Indian products can now be delivered to your doorstep; here is a list of good internet sites and mail order companies.

INTERNET GROCERS

Chilli-willie.co.uk
indiaspices.com (US)
QualitySpices.com
seasonedpioneers.com
Sweetmart.co.uk
thespiceoflife.co.uk
Thespicestore.com (US)

MAIL ORDER

Curry Club Direct Supplies
Tel/Fax: 01746 761211

Fox's Spices
Mason's Road Industrial Estate
Stratford-upon-Avon
Warwickshire
CV37 9NF
Tel: 01789 266420
Fax: 01789 267737

Natco Spices
Choithram House
Lancelot Road
Wembley
Middlesex
HA0 2BG
Tel: 020 8903 8311
Fax: 020 8900 1426

World Foods Cardiff
181 Penarth Road
Grangetown
Cardiff
CF11 6JW
Tel: 02920 394618

INDEX